符号中国 SIGNS OF CHINA

中国名湖

FAMOUS LAKES IN CHINA

"符号中国"编写组◎编著

中央民族大学出版社
China Minzu University Press

图书在版编目(CIP)数据

中国名湖 ：汉文、英文 / “符号中国”编写组编著. — 北京：
中央民族大学出版社, 2024.3

（符号中国）

ISBN 978-7-5660-2288-2

Ⅰ. ①中… Ⅱ. ①符… Ⅲ. ①湖泊－介绍－中国－汉、英 Ⅳ. ①K928.43

中国国家版本馆CIP数据核字（2024）第016963号

符号中国：中国名湖 FAMOUS LAKES IN CHINA

编　　著　“符号中国”编写组
策划编辑　沙　平
责任编辑　李苏幸
英文指导　李瑞清
英文编辑　邱　械
美术编辑　曹　娜　郑亚超　洪　涛
出版发行　中央民族大学出版社
　　　　　北京市海淀区中关村南大街27号　　邮编：100081
　　　　　电话：（010）68472815（发行部）　传真：（010）68933757（发行部）
　　　　　　　　（010）68932218（总编室）　　　　（010）68932447（办公室）
经 销 者　全国各地新华书店
印 刷 厂　北京兴星伟业印刷有限公司
开　　本　787 mm×1092 mm　1/16　印张：10
字　　数　128千字
版　　次　2024年3月第1版　2024年3月第1次印刷
书　　号　ISBN 978-7-5660-2288-2
定　　价　58.00元

“符号中国”丛书编委会

唐兰东　巴哈提　杨国华　孟靖朝　赵秀琴

本册编写者

韦　茗

前言 Preface

湖泊是“陆上的海”，是孕育和滋养人类文明的摇篮，人类千万年来都在受着她的恩泽。中国是一个湖泊众多的国家，共有湖泊两万多个。这些湖泊在中国版图上星罗棋布，像粒粒璀璨的珍珠散落在华夏大地上。中

Lakes are considered "oceans on land" and have always served as a cradle that nurtures and nourishes human civilization benefiting the mankind over the past millions of years. China is a country abundant in over 20,000 lakes scattered all over the vast land. Literati in ancient China compared water to bright

国古代文人湖畔行吟：“水是眼波横，山是眉峰聚。”湖泊就像人类的眼睛一般充满着睿智、生机和灵气。或仰卧在平原，或依偎在海滨，或镶嵌在雪山，或沉睡在深谷，姿态万千的湖泊景观各不相同，带给人类无限的美的享受。

本书以生动的文字、优美的插图，详细介绍了中国湖泊的成因和类型，以及著名的湖泊和它们所孕育的文化，可以让人们在学习了解地理知识的同时，也能在轻松愉悦中感受中国湖泊的妩媚多姿和积蕴深厚的人文魅力。

eyes and mountain peaks to eyebrows of a beautiful woman. Lakes were described as human eyes full of vitality and wisdom. A great variety of lake sceneries on the plains, by the sea, in snow mountains or deep valleys bring people enormous enjoyment of infinite beauty.

Illustrated with beautiful photos, this book provides a detailed and vivid account of different types of lakes, their formation, and culture bred around famous lakes. Readers can learn about the lakes' geological knowledge and at the same time appreciate a charming variety of lakes in China and their deeply embedded culture.

目 录 Contents

中国湖泊
Lakes in China 001

各地名湖
Famous Lakes 013

构造湖
Tectonic Lakes 014

火山口湖
Crater Lakes 082

堰塞湖
Barrier Lakes 085

冰川湖
Glacial Lakes 100

河成湖
Fluvial Lakes 106

海成湖
Shoreline Lakes 112

人工湖
Artificial Lakes 121

中国湖泊

Lakes in China

中国地域辽阔，湖泊分布范围广而不均，往往成群分布。中国有五大湖区，即东部湖区、东北湖区、蒙新湖区、青藏高原湖区和云贵高原湖区。由于所处的地理环境不同，湖泊在形成、发展、变迁的过程中受到自然和人为因素的不同影响，类型也变得多种多样，从而呈现出更加多种多样的形态。

Lakes are distributed widely, but unevenly in the vast land of China. However, they are relatively clustered in five big lake regions: the East Lakes Region, the Northeast Lakes Region, Inner Mongolia–Xinjiang Lakes Region, Qinghai–Tibet Plateau Lakes Region and Yunnan–Guizhou Plateau Lakes Region. Under different geographical environments, local natural and human factors contributed to the lake formation, development and vicissitude, which resulted in multiple lake types.

中国湖泊数量众多，分布广泛，按照其成因可分为构造湖、火山口湖、堰塞湖、冰川湖、喀斯特湖、风成湖、河成湖、海成湖和人工湖等几类。

构造湖是因地壳构造运动使地面凹陷积水而形成的湖泊。中国的

Lakes of China are numerous and widespread, according to their causes can be divided into several categories, including tectonic lakes, crater lakes, barrier lakes, glacial lakes, karst lakes, aeolian lakes, fluvial lakes, shoreline lakes and artificial lakes.

Tectonic or rift lakes form as water accumulates in the depression caused by fault movements of the earth crust. Most large and medium-size lakes in China belong to this category, such as the Dianchi Lake and Erhai Lake in the Yunnan Plateau, Namtso in the Qinghai-Tibet Plateau, Hulun Lake and Buir Lake

• **兴凯湖**

兴凯湖位于黑龙江省密山县，湖身呈椭圆形，总面积约4380 平方千米。湖边芦苇起伏摇曳，别具风情。

Khanka Lake

Khanka Lake is situated in Mishan County, Heilongjiang Province covering a total of 4,380 square kilometers with enchanting scenery of lakeside reeds.

湖光岩（图片提供：FOTOE）

湖光岩位于广东省湛江市西南部，面积2.3平方千米，水深20多米。湖水清澈，明净如镜。

Huguang Maar

Huguang Maar is situated in Zhanjiang City, Guangdong Province covering a total of 2.3 square kilometers with a depth of over 20 meters. The water is clear as a mirror.

大中型湖泊多属于这一类型，如云贵高原的滇池、洱海，青藏高原的纳木错，内蒙古高原的呼伦湖、贝尔湖，长江中下游地区的洞庭湖、鄱阳湖、巢湖以及中俄边境上的兴凯湖。

火山口湖是火山停止喷发后，火山口内积水而形成的湖泊，通常面积较小而深度较长。长白山地区是典型的火山地貌区域，主峰上的

in the Inner Mongolian Plateau, Dongting Lake, Poyang Lake and Chaohu Lake along the midstream and downstream of the Yangtze River as well as Khanka Lake located on the border between Russia and China.

Crater lakes form in a volcanic caldera as precipitation within the rim fills the crater after the volcano has been inactive for some time. A crater lake usually has a relatively smaller area and

天池是中国最大的火山口湖，湖水最深处达373米，也是中国最深的湖泊。广东的湖光岩、西樵山火口湖，台湾的大屯火山口湖也是火山口湖的代表。

堰塞湖是河道因山崩、地震、滑坡、泥石流或火山熔岩流阻塞而形成的湖泊。它们通常为地震、风灾、火山爆发等自然原因所造成，

a considerable depth. Heavenly Lake at the main peak of the typical volcanic Changbai Mountain Range is the largest crater lake in China with a maximum depth of 373 meters, the deepest of all lakes in China. Other typical crater lakes include Huguang Maar and Mount Xiqiao Crater Lake in Guangdong Province, and Datun Crater Lake in Taiwan Province.

Barrier lakes form as a result of

- **达里诺尔湖**（图片提供：全景正片）

达里诺尔湖位于内蒙古克什克腾旗，呈海马形状，面积238平方千米。

Darryl Lake

Situated in Hexigten, Inner Mongolia, the seahorse-shaped Darryl Lake covers 238 square kilometers.

也有人为因素如炸药爆破、工程挖掘等造就出来的堰塞湖。中国的堰塞湖主要有两类，一类是火山堰塞湖，如东北的镜泊湖、五大连池和内蒙古的达里诺尔湖等；另一类是因地震、冰川或泥石流而形成的堰塞湖，如藏东南的易贡错和汶川大地震造成的唐家山堰塞湖。

冰川湖是由冰川挖蚀成的洼地和冰碛物堵塞冰川槽谷积水而形成

• **新路海**（图片提供：全景正片）

新路海位于四川德格县境内，水源主要由雀儿山冰川和积雪消融供给，海拔4040米，平均水深约10米。

Yulong La-tso (Xinluhai Lake)

Yulong La-tso is located in Dege County, Sichuan Province, mainly fed by melted snow from Chola Mountain glaciers. It has an elevation of 4,040 meters and the average depth of 10 meters.

landslides, mudslides or lava blocking the river bed or valley as water accumulates to a certain level. Their formation is usually caused by natural factors, such as earthquakes, windstorms, volcano eruptions and sometimes human factors such as engineering mining and explosives. There are mainly two types of barrier lakes in China: volcanic lakes such as Jingpo Lake and Five Connected Lakes (*Wudaliangchi*) in northeast China, and Darryl Lake in Inner Mongolia; and barrier lakes caused by earthquakes, mudslides, landslides or glacier flows such as Yiong Tso Lake in southeast Xizang and Tangjiashan Barrier Lake as a result of a major earthquake in Wenchuan County, Sichuan Province.

Glacial lakes originate in melted glaciers. A retreating glacier often leaves behind large deposits of moraine in hollows between drumlins and they

的一类湖泊。中国冰川湖多为山谷冰川所形成，如青藏高原上的帕桑错，它位于念青唐古拉山和喜马拉雅山区，海拔3460米，长13千米，宽2千米，深60米，面积达26平方千米。四川甘孜的新路海，由冰蚀挖深、冰碛物堵塞河谷出口而成。新疆境内的一些冰川湖，大

melt to create lakes. Most glacial lakes in China come from glacier valleys such as Pasang Tso Lake between the Nyainqentanglha Mountain and the Himalayas at the Qinghai-Tibet Plateau. At an altitude of 3,460 meters, Pasang Tso Lake is 13 kilometers long, 2 kilometers wide and 60 meters deep, covering an area of 26 square kilometers.

喀斯特湖（图片提供：全景正片）
Karst Lake

多是冰期前的构造谷地，在冰期时受冰川强烈挖蚀，形成宽坦的槽谷，冰退时，槽谷受冰碛垄阻塞形成长形湖泊，如阿尔泰山脚下的喀纳斯湖。

喀斯特湖是由于碳酸盐类地层经流水的长期溶解产生了洼地或漏斗，当这些洼地或漏斗中的落水洞

Yulong La-tso (Xinluhai Lake) in Ganzi (Garzê), Sichuan Province is also a moraine lake. Some of the glacial lakes in Xinjiang originally were tectonic basins before the ice age. During the ice age, they went through glacial erosion processes and became wide trough valleys. When the glacial flow retreated, a long narrow lake formed as a result of moraines left behind blocking the outflow of melted ice in the valley. The formation of Kanas Lake at the foot of the Altai Mountains in Xinjiang is a good example.

Karst lakes come from depressions or sinkholes as a result of dissolution over a long period of layers of soluble bedrocks. These rocks are usually carbonate rocks such as limestone or dolomite. When the funnel of the depression is clogged, the inflow of spring water accumulates and forms the lake. Karst lakes are generally fed by stable underground water. Some of the Karst lakes are connected to underground river streams. They appear during the raining season and disappear when the water flows back into the underground streams in the dry season. Karst lakes in China are mainly distributed in Karst landforms in Guizhou Province, Guangxi Zhuang Autonomous

被堵塞后，泉水流入其中而形成，又称“岩溶湖”。喀斯特湖主要靠地下水供给，水量一般较为稳定。也有的喀斯特湖与地下河相通，只在雨季时出现，干旱季节湖水流入地下河而消失。中国的喀斯特湖主要集中分布在喀斯特地貌发育的贵州、广西、云南等省区，如贵州毕节的“三大连湖”——东风湖、索风湖、支嘎阿鲁湖。

风成湖是因沙漠中沙丘间的洼地低于潜水面，由四周潜水汇集洼地而形成。由于它瞬息万变，常常被称为“神出鬼没的湖泊”。风成湖滨牧草茂密，水源充足，是优良的天然牧场，因此成为沙漠地区人民劳动生息的地方。如敦煌附近的月牙湖，是泉水汇集形成的一个湖，湖水清澈见底，绿如翡翠，四周被沙山环绕，水面酷似一弯新月，月牙湖因此而得名。

河成湖的形成与河流的演变有密切关系。比如湖北的洪湖和河北的白洋淀，就是因为河流泥沙在平原上堆积不均匀，造成天然堤之间的洼地积水而形成。还有的河成湖是由于支流的水不能汇入干流，甚

Region and Yunnan Province. For example, the three connected lakes—Dongfeng Lake, Suofeng Lake and Zhiga A' lu Lake in Bijie, Guizhou Province—are such Karst lakes.

When depressions amidst the desert dunes are lower than the groundwater level, the water gathers in these basins and forms aeolian lakes. Known as "haunted lakes", the ever-changing aeolian lakes tend to appear and disappear quickly. Areas surrounding aeolian lakes are excellent natural grazing ground for people living in the desert thanks to the lush pasture and abundant water resources. Yueya Lake (Crescent Moon Lake) near Dunhuang of Gansu Province is such a place with crystal-clear water surrounded by sand hills. Yueya Lake is named after the crescent moon shape of the lake.

The formation of fluvial lakes is closely related to river course changes. For example, the Honghu Lake in Hubei Province and Baiyang Lake of Hebei Province came into being when river sediment piled up on the plain unevenly allowing water to accumulate between natural river banks. Some fluvial lakes form due to the fact that river tributaries are unable to enter the

• **月牙泉**（图片提供：全景正片）

月牙泉位于甘肃省敦煌市，古称“沙井”，南北长约100米，东西宽约25米。泉在沙漠中，从未干涸，从未被流沙掩盖，因此被称为沙漠奇观。

Yueya (Crescent Moon) Spring

Yueya Spring is located in Dunhuang City, Gansu Province. It was called a "sand well" in ancient times. It is 100-meter long from south to north and 25-meter wide from east to west. It is known as a wonder in the desert because the spring fountain has never been dried or covered by quicksand.

main stream, but instead the mainstream flows back to tributaries, which result in water accumulation. In addition, some lakes come from abandoned ancient watercourses as water is easily accumulated in these places.

A shoreline lake or a lagoon used to be an inner bay, which was gradually separated from the ocean and eventually

至干流水倒灌入支流而壅水成湖。此外，废弃古河道上的积水也极易形成河成湖。

海成湖又称“潟湖”，原系海湾，湾口处泥沙沉积，使海湾与海洋逐渐分离而形成湖泊。杭州西湖

became a lake as the sediment silted up the mouth of the bay. West Lake *Xi Hu* formed as sediment carried into the lagoon through inlets by the tide was constantly deposited near the bay mouth, which eventually separated the bay from the sea, and the seawater within the secluded

• **湖北武汉东湖**（图片提供：全景正片）

East Lake in Wuhan, Hubei Province

- **台湾高雄港**（图片提供：全景正片）

高雄港位于台湾省高雄市，长12千米，宽1—1.5千米，酷似一只口袋。湾内水深港阔，是一个天然良港。

Port of Kaohsiung, Taiwan Province

Port of Kaohsiung is located in Kaohsiung City, Taiwan Province. It is 12 kilometers long and 1-1.5 kilometers wide. Its shape resembles a pocket. It is a natural harbor with deep water and a broad port.

就是由于海潮和河流挟带的泥沙不断在湾口附近沉积，使海湾与海洋完全分离，海水慢慢淡化而形成的。台湾省西南岸的高雄港也是一个典型的海成湖。

人工湖是指人们为了消除水害、发展经济和交通而兴建的水

bay gradually desalinated. The Port of Kaohsiung at the southwest coast of Taiwan Province is a typical shoreline lake.

Artificial lakes are reservoirs or impoundments by deliberate human excavation for the purposes of water conservation, flood elimination,

• 北京北海
Beihai Lake in Beijing

库或者蓄水池。它主要用于拦洪蓄水，也可以用来灌溉、发电、养鱼。如吉林省的松花湖就是为了发电需要而在松花江上建造的大型水库。还有一种人工湖是以一种园林景观的形式存在的。

economic development and transportation constructions. They are mainly used for flood control, and for irrigation, power generation and fish farming as well. For example, Songhua Lake in Jilin Province is a large reservoir built on the Songhua River to generate electricity. Another type of artificial lakes was built as part of the garden landscape.

各地名湖
Famous Lakes

中国湖泊众多，面积在1平方千米以上的天然湖泊达2800多个，总面积约8万平方千米。本章按照湖泊的不同类型，对中国各地的名湖逐一介绍。大大小小的湖泊，形状各异，姿态万千。

China is rich in lakes. There are over 2,800 natural lakes covering a total of 80,000 square kilometers, each with an area of 1 square kilometer and more. This chapter introduces famous lakes of different types and shapes in different locations of China.

> 构造湖

呼伦湖

呼伦湖是一个构造断裂湖，位于内蒙古呼伦贝尔市，是内蒙古第一大湖。它原来被称为“大泽”“俱伦泊”，直到近代才被称为“呼伦湖”。湖周长447千米，湖面面积达2315平方千米，蓄水量为138.5亿立方米，水域宽广，碧波万顷，像一颗晶莹剔透的明珠镶嵌于呼伦贝尔大草原上，养育着无数草原儿女。

在1亿3500万年前，亚欧板块受太平洋板块挤压向东南方向滑动，现在的呼伦贝尔地区在强烈的挤压作用下沉降下去，于是，低洼处积水成湖。后来又由于地壳的运动，古湖盆的东西两侧出现两条大的断

> Tectonic Lakes

Hulun Lake

Hulun Lake is a tectonic lake located in Hulunbuir City, Inner Mongolia. It is the largest lake in Inner Mongolia. Originally it was called *Daze, Julunpo* and became known as Hulun Lake in modern times. The lake has a circumference of 447 kilometers, an area of 2,315 square kilometers and a water storage capacity of 13.85 billion cubic meters. This vast and crystal-clear lake has nurtured numerous families on the Hulunbeir prairie.

Over 135 million years ago, the Eurasian plate slid towards southeast under the pressure from the Pacific Ocean plate. Such strong crustal movement resulted in the depression of current Hulunbuir region. A lake formed as water accumulated in low-lying areas. Later two huge faults appeared on both the east

呼伦湖
Hulun Lake

裂带，湖盆继续下陷，形成今天的呼伦湖。

呼伦湖是北方游牧民族成长、发展的摇篮。据史料记载，这里是中国北方游牧民族的祖先游猎和生活的地方。近年来，考古工作者在湖泊周围挖掘出了猛犸象、披毛

and west side of the ancient lake basin due to further crustal movements. As a result continuous subsidence of the basin created today's Hunlun Lake.

Hulun Lake is considered the cradle of the growth and development of the nomadic people in the north. According to historical records, early nomads of

犀、东北野牛、转角羚羊等古生物化石和骨制鱼叉、鱼镖等大量的细石器。东汉时期（25—220），居住在这里的鲜卑人与中原地区商贸往来频繁，古墓葬中出土的大量文物便是最好的证据。

初春时节，位于中蒙边境的贝尔湖里的鱼群会顺着乌尔逊河拥进呼伦湖，形成鱼潮。这是一道双湖鱼跃的独特风景。夏秋之际，草原色彩最为浓烈，牛羊成群，生机无

north China lived and hunted in this place. In recent years, archaeologists excavated around the lake and discovered fossils of mammoths, woolly rhinoceros, northeast wild buffaloes and Topi antelopes as well as a large number of microliths such as harpoons and fishing spears made of bones. Many cultural relics unearthed from ancient tombs have proved that the Xianbei, an Asian Mongoloids population had frequent trading with people from China's Central

• 呼伦贝尔大草原
Hulunbuir Steppe

新巴尔虎蒙古族男儿三艺

新巴尔虎蒙古族男儿三艺是指摔跤、赛马、射箭。摔跤是两人力量与技能的综合较量，参赛者可尽情发挥，使用推、拉、勾、绊、提、压等各种技能，但不可触头、抱腿、击身，只要一方膝盖以上部位触地，对方就算获胜。赛马的比赛形式多种多样，有跑马、走马、颠马、驯马、套马、马术等，参赛者一般是少年。射箭分为步射和骑射，骑射即弓箭手骑马奔驰，在规定的时间内，射左右三个靶桩，这是最能体现射手射箭水平的方式。

Three Techniques of New Barag Mongolian Men

The three techniques of New Barag Mongolian men refer to wrestling, horse racing and archery. Wrestling is a contest of strength and skills between two men. Contestants can use a variety of skills including pushing, pulling, hooking, tripping and pressing, but are not allowed to touch the other wrestler's head, hold his legs or hit his body. A wrestler loses if he touches the ground with any part of his body above the knees. Horse racing competitions include racing, cantering, galloping, training and haltering a horse as well as other equestrian events. Horse racing participants are generally juvenile. Archery is competed on foot or on the horseback. The contestants on the horseback must hit three targets on both left and right side within a predetermined time. This is a contest that can best demonstrate the skills of the archer.

• **呼伦湖畔的新巴尔虎蒙古族村落**（图片提供：FOTOE）

New Barag Mongolian Village beside the Hulun Lake

限，草地上鲜花缤纷，湖中碧水微澜，鱼跃鸟飞，俨然构成一幅色彩美妙的图画。

生活在呼伦湖畔的新巴尔虎蒙古人非常注重礼仪，不论是否认识，见面都会问候“你好”“全家好”“草场好”之类的话语。如果有人来家里做客，不管相识与否，主人都会热情招待，先敬上一碗奶茶，再拿出糖块、点心、奶干等来招待。晚上如需住宿，主人则会亲自铺好被褥。新巴尔虎蒙古人对长者十分敬重，与老年人相见时，必须衣帽整洁；如果在野外遇见老人，则需要下马或下车请安问好；青年人不可与老人一起饮酒，也不可与其平坐。

微山湖

微山湖位于山东济宁的微山县，是山东省第一大淡水湖，与昭阳湖、独山湖、南阳湖彼此相连，被称为“南四湖”。南四湖中以微山湖面积最大，所以统称“微山湖”。关于微山湖名字的来历，可追溯到商代。商纣王沉迷酒色，暴虐无道。他的哥哥微子（名启）

Plain during the East Han Dynasty (25-220).

In early spring, large quantities of fish stocks from the Buir Lake on the border between China and Mongolia migrate via the Orxon River into Hulun Lake creating a unique scene of fish tides in both places. Between summer and autumn, the Hulunbuir Steppe displays a spectacular picture of cattle and sheep flocks, colorful wild flowers, flying birds and jumping fish in the lake's green and clear water.

New Barag Mongolians living around Hulun Lake pay great attention to etiquette. They greet friends and strangers alike with "how are you", "how is your family" or "how is your pasture". When someone visits their home, whether they know the person or not, the host will treat the visitor warmly by presenting a cup of milk tea served with candies and cookies. If the visitor needs to stay overnight, the host family will have a bed prepared. Xin Barag Mongolians respect the elderly deeply. They will dress up for a meeting with an elderly. If they see an elder person outside, they will get off their horse to greet the person. Young people are not allowed to drink with the elderly or to sit with the elderly side by side.

微山湖荷塘（图片提供：FOTOE）
Lotus Pond of Weishan Lake

微山湖（图片提供：FOTOE）
Weishan Lake

数次向他进谏都没有被采纳，于是愤然出走隐居在微山岛上，死后葬于此地。人们为了纪念微子，便把湖命名为微山湖。

微山湖是在燕山构造运动的影响下，下陷积水而形成的，南北长150千米，东西最宽处达25千米，水域面积达664平方千米。微山湖承纳

Weishan Lake

Weishan Lake is situated in Weishan County of Jining, Shandong Province. It is the biggest freshwater lake of Shandong interconnecting with Weishan Lake, Zhaoyang Lake, Dushan Lake and Nanyang Lake, known as the Southern Four Lakes. Together these four lakes are

• 微山岛上的微子墓（图片提供：FOTOE）
Tomb of Weizi on Weishan Island

了鲁、苏、皖、豫四省区的来水，有40多条河水汇流湖中，形成了中国北方最大的淡水湖。京杭大运河纵贯全湖，无论南下苏杭，还是北上京津，都可畅通无阻，是中国重要的黄金水道。

微山湖景色优美，湖中遍植荷花，多达万亩。每至盛夏，湖

generally referred to as Weishan Lakes since Weishan Lake covers the largest area. The history of the name "Weishan" can be traced back to the Shang Dynasty. The extreme decadence and tyranny of King Zhou of Shang made his brother Weizi walk away from his regime after Weizi's suggestions were rejected many times. Weizi then lived a seclude life and was buried on Weishan Island. The lake was named Weishan Lake in memory of Weizi.

Weishan Lake formed as a result of water accumulation in the depression caused by tectonic movements of Mount Yanshan. It is 150 kilometers long from south to north and 25 kilometers wide from east to west with a lake surface area of 664 square kilometers. Water from over 40 rivers in Shandong, Jiangsu, Anhui and Henan provinces converges at Weishan Lake making it the largest freshwater lake in North China. It is also considered a "golden waterway" of China as the Beijing-Hangzhou Grand Canal runs through the lake supporting the transportation to Suzhou, Hangzhou in the south and Beijing, Tianjin in the north.

Well-known for its scenic beauty, Weishan Lake has over 1,647 acres of

面上花团锦簇，荷香四溢，沁人心脾，因此得名“中国荷都”。

微山岛位于微山湖西南部，是微山湖中最大的岛屿。岛上有三贤墓：微子墓、目夷墓、张良墓。张良墓是三座墓中最大的一座。张良（？—前189或前190）是秦末汉初杰出的军事家，曾经帮助汉高祖刘邦夺得天下，建立汉王朝。刘邦称赞他“运筹帷幄之中，决胜千里之外”。其墓前有清乾隆二年(1737年) 所立的石碑，上书“汉留侯张良墓”。此外，这里还出土了大量精美的汉画像石刻和古碑，充分显示了这一地区的悠久历史和繁荣的文化。

大明湖

大明湖位于山东济南市中心偏东北处，是“中国第一泉水湖”，与趵突泉、千佛山同为济南三大名胜。这是一个由城内众泉汇流而成的天然湖泊，故有“众泉汇流”之说。湖水面积约0.465平方千米，平均水深2米，最深处约4米。大明湖已有1400多年的历史，北魏地理学家郦道元（约470—527）在其撰写

lotuses. In midsummer, the lake presents a spectacle of blooming lotus flowers with refreshing fragrance winning the reputation as "the capital of lotus flowers in China".

To the southwest of Weishan Lake is Weishan Island, the largest island in the lake. There are three tombs for noted personalities on the island: Weizi Tomb, Muyi Tomb and Zhang Liang Tomb, the largest of the three. Zhang Liang (?-189 or 190 B.C.) was a famous military strategist between the late Qin Dynasty and the beginning of the Han Dynasty. He assisted Emperor Liu Bang of the Han Dynasty in the struggle to dominate China and was highly commended by Emperor Liu Bang for his ability of "wining battles thousands of miles away by strategizing in a military tent". A stele was built in front of his tomb with the inscription from Emperor Qianlong of the Qing Dynasty in 1737. Many cultural relics including exquisite Han stone carvings of portraits and steles have demonstrated the long history and flourishing culture of this region.

Daming Lake

Daming Lake is located in the northeast of Jinan City, Shangdong Province.

的地理著作《水经注》中称大明湖为“陂”“历水”，唐时称“莲子湖”，宋代称“四望湖”，后被金代文学家元好问称为“大明湖”，之后沿用至今。

大明湖自然风景秀美，一湖烟水，景色秀丽。湖中种有40多亩荷花，每至夏季，湖面上莲花盛开，红荷绿蒲，十分美丽。“四面荷花三面柳，一城山色半城湖”，成为大明湖风景的最好写照。

大明湖畔有多处名胜古迹，其中以历下亭、铁公祠最为有名。历

Known as the "No.1 spring water lake in China", it is one of the three cultural landmarks of Jinan with Baotu (Spouting) Spring and Mount Qianfo (Mount Thousand Buddha). It is said that the lake formed when spring water from all over the city converged at this location. The lake's surface area is 0.465 square kilometers and 2 meters deep on average with the maximum depth of 4 meters. The lake has a history of over 1,400 years. Li Daoyuan (approx. 470-527), a geographer in the Northern Wei Dynasty called it "*Bei*" (pond) and "*Li Shui*" (traveling water) in his classic of

大明湖风光（图片提供：全景正片）
Scenery of Daming Lake

下亭位于大明湖最大的湖心岛上，因南临历山而得名，有“中国第一古亭”之称。亭子挺拔端庄，古朴典雅，红柱青瓦，八角重檐，雕梁画栋，是一座轩昂古雅的木结构建筑。亭身空透，亭下四周有木制坐栏，亭内有石雕莲花桌凳，以供游人休憩。亭中匾额上的“历下亭”三字为清乾隆皇帝手书。亭北名士轩的墙上嵌有唐代杜甫、李邕的石刻画像及济南历代名人的画像，门前抱柱上刻有中国著名文学家郭沫若撰写的对联“杨柳春风万方极乐，芙渠秋月一片大明”。

铁公祠坐落在大明湖北岸西端，建于清乾隆五十七年（1792年），是为纪念明代兵部尚书、山东参政铁铉而建。铁公祠呈长方形，占地近7000平方米。东大门为朱红色锁壳式门楼，迎门有太湖石，屹立于松荫之中。大门以北，是半壁曲廊，廊壁上辟有花窗，框出幅幅小景。

巢湖

巢湖，古称“南巢”，是中国第五大淡水湖。巢湖位于安徽省中

Commentary about Waterways. The lake was known as "the Lotus Lake" in the Tang Dynasty and "Siwang Lake" (Lake of Four Directions) in the Song Dynasty. Yuan Haowen, a literary figure of the Jin Dynasty named it Daming Lake and since then the name has been used till the present day.

Daming Lake has an enchanting natural beauty. Red lotus flowers blossom in green leaves on a pond of 6.6 acres making the summer time the most beautiful season. Such scenery is best described in a poem as, "Lotus flowers on four directions along with green willow trees on three sides; the splendid landscape of the entire city contributing to the lake covering half of the city."

Daming Lake is surrounded by many historical landmarks and buildings, among which Lixia Pavilion and the Temple of Lord Tie (*Tiegong Ci*) are the most famous. Located in the largest central lake island (Huxin Island), Lixia Pavilion was named after the neighboring Lishan Mountain to the south. Known as the "No. 1 ancient pavilion in China", it is an elegant classic wood structure with red columns, dark green tiles and an octagonal double-eave roof of painted beams. Open all around, the pavilion has

• 历下亭（图片提供：全景正片）
Lixia Pavilion

部合肥、巢湖、肥西、肥东、庐江等市县之间。据地质学家考证，巢湖是由于地层局部陷落积水而形成的。大约在距今两亿年前，地壳运动使陆地上升，海水残留在内陆凹陷部分，巢湖就是当时形成的。巢湖湖型狭长，东西长54.5千米，南北宽15.1千米，湖岸线总长184.66千米，面积769.5平方千米。自空中俯瞰，犹如一只巨大的鸟巢，故名“巢湖”。

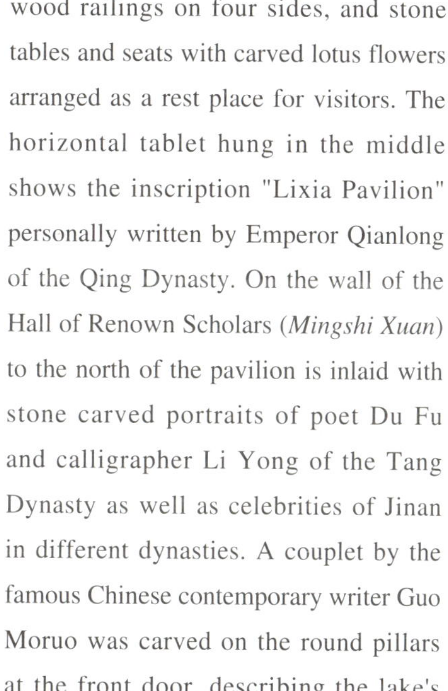

wood railings on four sides, and stone tables and seats with carved lotus flowers arranged as a rest place for visitors. The horizontal tablet hung in the middle shows the inscription "Lixia Pavilion" personally written by Emperor Qianlong of the Qing Dynasty. On the wall of the Hall of Renown Scholars (*Mingshi Xuan*) to the north of the pavilion is inlaid with stone carved portraits of poet Du Fu and calligrapher Li Yong of the Tang Dynasty as well as celebrities of Jinan in different dynasties. A couplet by the famous Chinese contemporary writer Guo Moruo was carved on the round pillars at the front door, describing the lake's enchanting scenery in the spring and the fall.

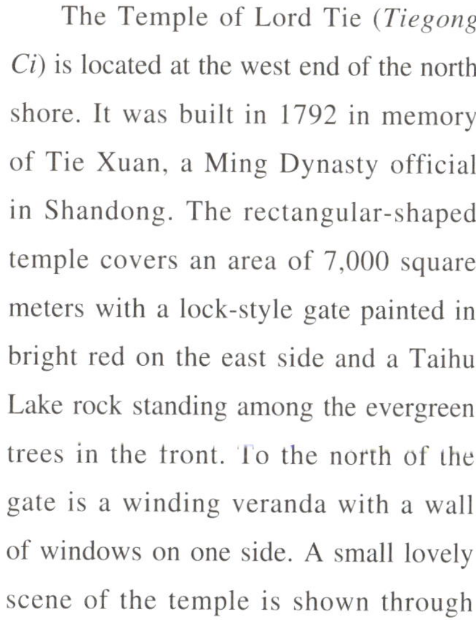

The Temple of Lord Tie (*Tiegong Ci*) is located at the west end of the north shore. It was built in 1792 in memory of Tie Xuan, a Ming Dynasty official in Shandong. The rectangular-shaped temple covers an area of 7,000 square meters with a lock-style gate painted in bright red on the east side and a Taihu Lake rock standing among the evergreen trees in the front. To the north of the gate is a winding veranda with a wall of windows on one side. A small lovely scene of the temple is shown through

姥山位于巢湖湖中央，面积不足1平方千米。山顶有座著名的文峰塔，又名“望儿塔”。此塔始建于明代崇祯年间，塔共7层，135级，

• 《巢湖图》石涛（清）
Chaohu Lake by Shitao(Qing Dynasty, 1616-1911)

each of the windows on the wall as if they were framed pictures.

Chaohu Lake

Chaohu Lake, known as Southern Chao in ancient times, is the fifth largest freshwater lake in China. It is situated in central Anhui Province, among Heifei City, Chaohu City, Feixi County, Feidong County, and Lujiang City,etc. According to a geologist study, the lake formed as water accumulated in the depression caused by certain fault movements. About two hundred million years ago, strong rising of earth's crust left sea water in inland depressions, one of which became Chaohu Lake's basin. Long and narrow, the lake is 54.5 kilometers long from east to west, 15.1 kilometers wide from south to north covering an area of 769.5 square kilometers with a total circumference of 184.66 kilometers. In an aerial view, the shape of the lake resembles a bird nest, hence the name Chaohu (*Chao* means bird nest) Lake.

Mount Mushan is located in the center of the Chaohu Lake covering an

高51米。塔体呈八角形，飞檐翘角，用青砖垒砌而成。塔内有砖雕佛像802尊，塔壁每层都刻有古人诗歌和浮雕，十分美观。

巢湖之南，群峰相峙，其中银屏峰海拔508米，为群峰之首，与姥山遥遥相望。因山上有一块形如白色花瓶的大石，故又有“银瓶”之名。围绕银屏峰的九座山峰，形状如狮子，故名“九狮山”，古人称之为“九狮抱银瓶”。山麓有仙人洞，是由地下水溶蚀石灰岩形成的溶洞，洞内石笋、石柱形态各异，美不胜收。

四顶山亦称“四鼎山”，位于巢湖北岸，因有四峰突起而得名。据《巢湖志》记载，四顶山山顶以前有朝霞寺，寺周围古树葱茏，环境清幽。山上景色以霞光著称，日出或日落时分，满山被霞光染得光彩夺目，湖水闪闪发光，景色极为壮观。中庙，被称为“湖天第一胜境”，坐落于巢湖北岸凤凰台的矶石上。它三面临水，颇有气势。该庙为四合院式的纯木质结构，楼台高耸，精巧别致。

area of less than 1 square kilometer. At the peak of the mountain stands the famous Wenfeng Pagoda, also known as Wang'er (meaning hoping for son's return) Pagoda. Constructed during the Emperor Chongzhen's reigr of the Ming Dynasty, the 51-meter high octagonal pagoda built in dark green tiles has seven storeys and 135 stairs with upturned eaves and raised roof corners. There are 802 brick statues of Buddha in the pagoda. Every floor is decorated with beautiful reliefs and carvings of ancient poems.

To the south of Chaohu Lake stands a group of mountain peaks, of which Yinping (Silver Vase) Peak is the tallest at an elevation of 508 meters facing Mount Mushan in the distance. Named after a white big rock in the shape of a vase, Yinping Peak is surrounded by nine lion-shaped peaks known as "nine lion mountains". The scenery was described as "nine lions embracing a silver vase" in ancient times. At the foot of the mountain there is a limestone cave known as a "celestial cave" full of different shapes of stalagmites and stone columns.

Mount Siding (Mount Four Peaks) is situated at the northern shore of Chaohu Lake named after the four abruptly

姥山（图片提供：FOTOE）
Mount Mushan

太湖

太湖位于江苏和浙江两省的交界处，长江三角洲的南部，是中国第三大淡水湖，号称“三万六千顷，周围八百里”。早在多年以前，太湖地区受地壳运动影响而下陷，后积水成湖。整个太湖水系共有大小湖泊180多个，湖岸线总长405千米，平均水深1.89米。湖区有48岛、72峰，水域面积约为2420平方千米。

rising peaks. According to *Ancient Records of Chaohu Lake*, there was a temple named Zhaoxia (Morning Glow) Temple surrounded by ancient trees in a tranquil location at the top of Mount Siding famous for its splendid views of dazzling morning and sunset glow reflecting on the lake. Located on the cliff side of Phoenix Terrace (*Fenghuang Tai*) is Zhong Temple known as the "No. 1 attraction between the sky and the lake". Facing the water on three sides, this courtyard-style wooden structure at

太湖，东邻苏州，西接宜兴，南濒湖州，北临无锡。太湖流域是中国古代文明发源地之一。早在六七千年前，这里就有原始人类聚居。商朝末年，勾吴古国在此建立，后逐渐强大，成为“吴中胜地”。唐宋以来，太湖流域一直是中国著名的“鱼米之乡”和最为富庶的地区之一。

• 太湖
Taihu Lake

the top of the mountain has a magnificent and elegant appearance.

Taihu Lake

Taihu Lake situated to the south of the Yangtze Delta plain on the border between Jiangsu and Zhejiang provinces. It is the third largest freshwater lake in China known as having "an area of 36,000 *Qing* and 800 *Li* of shorelines" in ancient times (1 *Qing* ≈ 16.47 acres; 1 *Li*=500 meters). Many years ago, areas around Lake Tai sunk and became a basin as a result of crustal movement. The lake

• **碧螺春茶**

名列中国十大名茶之一的碧螺春产于太湖洞庭山。碧螺春属于绿茶，干茶色泽碧绿，形似螺壳，产于早春。冲泡成茶后，茶汤颜色嫩绿明亮，味道清香浓郁，饮后有回甜之感。

Biluochun (Green Spiral Spring) Tea

Biluochun Tea is one of the ten most famous green teas originally grown in Dongting Mountain of Taihu Lake. The spiral-shaped tea leaves have a very bright green color and the tea is picked in early spring. Brewed tea liquid shows a tender green color with a delicate floral aroma and leaves a sweet fruity taste in the mouth after drinking.

太湖中最大的岛是洞庭西山，它位于太湖的南部，面积62.5平方千米，它以群岛风光、花果丛林、吴越以来的古迹见长。洞庭西山山体主要为石灰岩，由于长期受侵蚀，怪石嶙峋，洞穴颇多。岛上的太湖石玲珑剔透，将全岛装点得十分别致。

formed as water in the basin accumulated. There are about 180 big and small ponds in the Taihu Lake water system of 405 kilometers long shorelines and an average depth of 1.89 meters. The lake has 48 islands and 78 mountain peaks covering a surface area of 2,420 square kilometers.

Taihu Lake faces Suzhou in the east, connects to Yixing in the west and borders Huzhou in the south and Wuxi in the north. It is considered one of the birthplaces of Chinese ancient civilization and inhabited by humans six or seven thousand years ago. The ancient state of Gouwu was established in this region at the end of the Shang Dynasty and became a powerful state acclaimed as the "best place on the Wu Plain". Since the Tang and Song dynasties, the Taihu Lake basin has always been one of the richest areas known as "the land of rice and fish" in China.

Situated to the south of Taihu Lake is Dongting Western Hill, the largest island on the lake covering 62.5 square kilometers of trees, floral shrubs and relics from Wuyue culture. These limestone hills are full of caves and grotesque rocks due to long time erosion. The exquisite Taihu Lake rocks have added a unique flavor to the landscape of the island.

太湖北岸有一块巨石伸入湖中，酷似畅饮湖水的神龟，于是得名“鼋头渚”。鼋头渚上建有涵虚亭，站在亭中观看太湖，水天相接，气势雄浑。岸边崖上镌刻着清代廖纶书写的“包孕吴越”和“横云”两组醒目的大字。广福寺建于1925年，矗立在峭壁顶端，颇有深山古寺之风。

邓尉山又名“光福山”“香雪海”，是斜插进太湖的一个半岛。

On the north shore a huge rock extends into the lake resembling a turtle drinking the water, hence the name Yuantou Island (Turtle Head Island). Hanxu Pavilion stands in the center of the island, presenting a magnificent view of the water totally immersing with the sky. Carved on the rocks along the shoreline are two huge inscriptions of "Breeding Wuyue" and "High Clouds". On the top of the precipitous cliff is Guangfu Temple built in 1925 with a style of an ancient temple hidden in the deep mountains.

• 太湖鼋头渚（图片提供：全景正片）
Yuantou Island in Taihu Lake

自古以来这里就是中国的赏梅胜地，相传清代的一名官员来到这里，看到梅花竞相开放，似海、似雪，触景生情写下“香雪海”三字。康熙皇帝、乾隆皇帝都曾到邓尉山赏梅并留下多首梅花诗，使“香雪海”名扬天下。

Mount Dengwei, also known as Mount Guangfu or *Xiangxuehai*, is a peninsula on the lake, which has always been the best location to see blooming plum blossom flowers. It is said that a Qing Dynasty official who came here was so struck by the blossom that he instantaneously wrote three characters "*Xiang Xue Hai*" meaning fragrance, snow and sea. Both Emperor Kangxi and Emperor Qianlong of the Qing Dynasty visited Mount Dengwei and left behind many poems about plum, making this place even more famous.

太湖石

太湖石，又称“窟窿石”“假山石”，从岩石学的角度来说，它是一种被溶蚀的石灰岩，因产于太湖而得名“太湖石”。它分为水石和干石。水石是长期受波浪冲击、溶蚀而形成；干石则是在酸性红壤中长期受侵蚀而形成的。太湖石具有“透”“瘦”“皱”“漏”等特点。“透”即石峰玲珑剔透；“瘦”即石体硬瘦苗条；“皱”即石体疏密得当；“漏”即石体九窍相通。太湖石多为灰色，因长期在大自然中受外来力量的侵蚀，久而久之，产生许多窝孔、穿孔、道孔，形状奇特而又圆润。

其实，太湖石并非只产于太湖，北京、山东、安徽等地也有出产。各地出产的太湖石虽有颜色、外形等差别，但因皆自然天成，棱角毕现，单独成景或叠为假山，都具有很高的欣赏价值，故而都是中国古典园林布景的最佳石材。太湖石早在唐朝时就已经闻名于世，中国许多皇家园林内都布置着太湖石景。

Taihu Lake Stones

Taihu Lake stones are also called "stones of holes" and "artificial mountain stones". In petrology, they are corroded limestones. Since they are produced in Taihu Lake, hence the name Taihu Lake stones. This kind of stones consists of two types: water rocks as a result of the solubility of limestone in water after a long period of impact from the waves; and dry rocks caused by long time acid erosion in red soil. They are characterized by delicate and slender shapes, proper distributed stone density and interconnected rock cracks and holes. Most Taihu Lake stones have a grayish color. Long-time natural erosion produces a variety of unique shapes of rock holes and cracks.

In fact, Taihu Lake stones are also produced in Beijing city, Shandong and Anhui provinces. Although they differ in color and shapes, they are all considered the best rockery for Chinese classical gardens. Their distinctive natural formation contains a very high value in artistic appreciation, whether they are used as a standalone landscape or built as artificial hills. Taihu Lake stones became famous as early as in the Tang Dynasty. Many Chinese imperial gardens are decorated with rock landscapes made from Taihu Lake stones.

• **太湖石"冠云峰"**

冠云峰现存苏州留园，该石"清""奇""顽""拙""透""瘦""皱""漏"八个字占全，尤其一个"皱"字，为它石所不及。

Cloud-capped Peak

The Cloud-capped peak is currently kept in the Lingering Garden, Suzhou City. This piece of stone meets all the criteria of "clear", "wonder", "naughty", "clumsy", "transparency", "slender", "wrinkle" and "hollow". Its "wrinkle" cannot be matched by any other stones.

鄱阳湖

鄱阳湖位于江西省上饶市，长达110千米，宽约70千米，是中国最大的淡水湖。全湖南宽北狭，犹如一只系在长江腰带上的宝葫芦。

大约在200万到300万年前，地球发生剧烈的新构造运动，九江一带陷落形成一个巨大的凹地。之后，凹地逐渐贮水，形成了巨大湖泊——彭蠡泽。在大冰期时，彭蠡泽面积大大缩小。距今6000到7000年前，全球进入冰期后的温暖时期，海水上升，海侵范围扩大，长江受海水抬升和顶托，在洼地积水。赣江的水流停积在原彭蠡泽区，逐渐形成今日的鄱阳湖。

鄱阳湖面因季节变化很大，春夏之交湖水猛涨，水面扩大，湖区广阔；冬季湖水剧降，水落石出，洲滩裸露，湖面仅剩几条蜿蜒的水道，因此有“洪水一片，枯水一线”之说。在鄱阳湖、长江汇合处景观奇特，一边混浊，一边清澈，互不相融，一条明显的清浊分界线清晰可观。

鄱阳湖湖区降水丰富，气候

Poyang Lake

Poyang Lake in Shangrao City of Jiangxi Province is the largest freshwater lake in China. At a length of 110 kilometers and a width of 70 kilometers, the lake is wider in the south and narrower in the north resembling a Chinese magic gourd tied on the Yangtze River.

Between two and three million years ago, violent crustal movements created a huge depression in the Jiujiang region. The water accumulation in the low-lying land formed a big lake of Pengli Marsh. During the Great Ice Age, Pengli Marsh was drastically reduced in size. Around 6,000 to 7,000 years ago after the ice age, the earth entered a period of warming, which caused water in the sea to rise and expand. As a result, the water in the Yangtze River rose and flooded many basins. The water from the Ganjiang River, a major tributary of the Yangtze River, accumulated in the Pengli Marsh and created today's Poyang Lake.

The surface area of Poyang Lake varies greatly in size due to seasonal changes. The lake expands broadly between the turn of spring and summer when water rises tremendously and shrinks drastically in winter when only

鄱阳湖（图片提供：全景正片）
Poyang Lake

温润，水草丰美。湖区聚集了许多世界珍稀濒危物种。每年冬季，大群的候鸟会来此越冬，因此湖区有“珍禽王国”之称。白鹤是世界濒临绝迹的物种，在鄱阳湖区有4000多只，是国内重要的白鹤栖息地。

在鄱阳湖不远处矗立着一座小岛，名“大孤山”，犹如漂浮在水面上的一只鞋，故又称“鞋山”。鞋山高出水面70多米，岛上林木苍郁，殿宇的天花宫坐落在此。位于

a few streams of water remain on a bare marshland. This phenomenon is described as "flooding all over or drying out in one stream". A distinct line dividing the clear from the muddy water is clearly visible at the location where the water from the Yangtze River and Poyang Lake converges.

Poyang Lake provides a wetland habitat for many world endangered species thanks to the warm and mild climate, abundant rainfalls and lush

湖口东南岸的石钟山，海拔不到50米，因山多罅穴，水石相击，声如洪钟，故名“石钟山”。石钟山雄奇秀丽，吸引了无数文人墨客来

aquatic plants. The lake is known as the "kingdom of rare birds". Every winter large groups of migratory birds fly to this place. Over 4,000 Siberian cranes, a world endangered species inhabit there.

Not very far from Poyang Lake is a small island called "Dagu Hill", which resembles a large shoe floating in the water and thus it is also called Shoe Hill. The Shoe Hill is more than 70 meters above the water covered with lush green trees. The magnificent Tianhua (Heavenly Flowers) Palace is situated on top of the hill. Mount Shizhong (Stone Bell) is located on the southeast shore of the lake at an elevation of no more than 50 meters. The name *Shizhong* is derived from the huge sound of water droplets falling on the stone. The enchanting scenery of Mount Shizhong attracted numerous Chinese literary figures to come for sightseeing. Su Shi, a famous writer and poet of the Song Dynasty paid a night visit here to study the history of its name and left behind a well-liked prose about Mount Shizhong. Mount Shizhong had always been a military battleground

• 石钟山（图片提供：FOTOE）
Mount Shizhong

此游历观赏，宋代大文豪苏轼就曾夜探石钟山，研究得名“石钟山”的缘由，并留下了脍炙人口的《石钟山记》。这里地势险要，历来是兵家必争之地，还发生过许多撼动人心的英雄故事。如三国时期的东吴名将周瑜（175—210）曾在此操练水师，明代开国皇帝朱元璋（1328—1398）与陈友谅的鄱阳湖之战也发生在这里。

because of its difficult terrain and strategic significance. It was also a place where many heroic stories took place. For example, the famous general Zhou Yu (175-210) of State Wu in the Three Kingdoms Period conducted navy drills here. The battle between Zhu Yuanzhang, the first emperor of the Ming Dynasty and Chen Youliang, a rebel leader at the end of the Yuan Dynasty also took place at Poyang Lake.

鄱阳湖文化

鄱阳湖地区历史悠久，文化繁荣。吴城遗址曾出土了较为完整的石器、陶器、青铜器、玉器、牙雕等，共900余件，是首次在江南地区发现的大规模人类居住的商代遗址。山背遗址出土了大批生产工具和生活用品，如锛、斧、镞、铲、凿、网坠、镰、球、砺石等，陶器有鼎、规鬲、豆、壶、罐、簋等。这些文物的出土对研究鄱阳湖地区的历史有重要的价值。

南昌是位于鄱阳湖地区的历史文化名城，距今已有2200余年的历史。汉高祖五年（前202），汉将灌婴奉命在当地驻军，修筑“灌城”，开创了南昌的建城历史。唐宋时，南昌已成为中国江南都会。名列江南三大名楼之首的滕王阁位于南昌市西北部赣江东岸，始建于唐代。主体建筑高57.5米，下部为12米台座，台座以上为主阁，共九层。玛瑙红大理石，青色琉璃瓦，绚烂华丽。唐代文学家王勃省父路过此地，即兴写下了《滕王阁序》，其中的名句“落霞与孤鹜齐飞，秋水与长天一色”生动描绘了这里的美景。

Culture of Poyang Lake

The Poyang Lake region enjoyed cultural prosperity in its long history. Over 900 pieces of relics including tools and utensils made of stone, pottery, bronze and jade as well as ivory carvings were unearthed in the ruins of Wucheng, which is the first Shang Dynasty site with large-scale human habitation discovered south of the Yangtze River. In addition, a large quantity of production tools and daily household items were also unearthed in the Shanbei ruins including adzes, axes, arrowheads, shovels, chisels, fish net sinkers, sickle, and balls as well as cooking utensils made of pottery. These cultural relics have important value in the study of the ancient Poyang Lake history.

Nanchang is a famous city of culture in the Poyang Lake region with a history of over 2, 200 years. Originally the city was built by Guan Ying, a general of the Han Dynasty stationed in the area and thus named "Guan City" at the time. By the Tang and Song dynasties, the city became a metropolitan area south of the Yangtze River. Tengwang Pavilion, one of the three famous buildings south of the Yangtze River, is located on the east shore of Gan River northwest of Nanchang. Tengwang Pavilion was built in the Tang Dynasty. The main structure is 57.5 meters high sitting on a 12-meter tall concrete platform with a total of nine storeys. The pavilion has a resplendent appearance in agate red marble and cyan glazed tiles. The beauty of Tengwang Pavilion inspired Wang Bo, a famous litterateur of the Tang Dynasty to write *Tengwang Pavilion Preface* when he passed through the location on his way to see his father. His famous verse described the sight as, "The sunset glow is flying together with a lonely wild goose, and the autumn water blends with the sky at the horizon."

• 滕王阁
Tengwang Pavilion

洞庭湖

洞庭湖，古称“云梦泽”，位于长江荆江河段以南，跨湖南、湖北两省。大约在两亿五千万年以前，洞庭湖区还是雪峰山脉的陷落部分，即断陷湖盆。由于这一带地势低洼曲折，长江和湘江、资水河、沅江、澧江四水流经此地，泥沙不断沉积，导致江水四溢，逐渐形成湖泊。湖中心有座小山，常年

Dongting Lake

Dongting Lake, known as "Yunmeng (Cloud Dream) Marsh" in ancient times, is located in the south of the Yangtze River's tributary Jingjiang River across both Hunan and Hubei provinces. About 250 million years ago, this area was a tectonic basin as a result of depressions in the nearby snow mountain ranges. Water from the Yangtze River, Xiangjiang River, Zishui River, Yuanjiang River

洞庭湖（图片提供：全景正片）
Dongting Lake

郁郁葱葱，名叫“洞庭山”，洞庭湖便因此得名。历史上的洞庭湖素有“八百里洞庭”之称，后来大量泥沙淤积湖底，使湖面面积逐渐缩小。现在湖区面积2740平方千米，是中国第二大淡水湖，中国第三大湖。

洞庭湖区风光卓绝，水天一色，胜迹无数。其中以湖中的君山和耸立在湖畔的岳阳楼最负盛名。

君山由大小72座山峰组成，呈椭圆形，是洞庭湖上的一个孤岛，

and Lijiang River all flowed through this low-lying land causing continuous sediment deposits which led to flooding and lake formations. Dongting Lake was named after a small evergreen mountain called Mount Dongting in the center of the lake. The lake had a reputation of being as long as 800 *Li* (1 *Li*=500 meters) in history, but gradually became smaller due to large sedimentation at the bottom of the lake. Dongting Lake is now the third largest lake and the second largest freshwater lake in China covering a total of 2,740 square kilometers.

• **洞庭湖君山的柳毅井**（图片提供：全景正片）

Liuyi Well on the Mount Junshan in Dongting Lake

古称“湘山”，又名“洞庭山”。由于这里山水相映，无比秀美，因此历代文人名士对其吟咏不绝。这里古迹遍布，如舜帝二妃墓。相传4000年前，舜帝南巡，他的两个妃子娥皇、女英追他到洞庭湖，不料被大风阻挡。此时她们忽然得到舜帝已死的消息，便抱竹痛哭，眼泪滴在竹上，变成竹上的斑点。不久，二人忧郁而死。人们为了纪念她们，修建了舜帝二妃墓。

君山还有许多名产奇珍，其中尤以有“金镶玉”之称的君山银针茶闻名，它自唐代起便被列为贡茶。君山银针内呈橙黄色，外裹一层白毫，冲泡之始，茶叶全部向上冲，继而徐徐下沉，最

• 君山银针茶样
Yinzhen (Silver Tip) Tea from Mount Junshan

There are numerous scenic attractions around Dongting Lake. Mount Junshan in the center of the lake and Yueyang Tower at the lakeside are the two most famous scenic spots.

Mount Junshan consists of 72 peaks on an oval-shaped island in Dongting Lake. It was called Mount Xiangshan in ancient times, also referred to as Mount Dongting. Generations of writers and poets left behind many literary works about Mount Junshan's scenic beauty. The island is full of historical sites such as the tomb of the two imperial concubines. It is said that 4,000 years ago during Emperor Shun's inspection visit in the south, two imperial concubines named Ehuang and Nvying followed him to Lake Dongting, but were stopped by stormy weather. When they heard the news that Emperor Shun had already passed away they cried so much that their teardrops turned the bamboo into mottled bamboo. Soon the two concubines died of overwhelming sadness and local people built a tomb on Mount Junshan in memory of them.

Mount Junshan also produces many local specialties among which the most famous is Yinzhen (Silver Tip) Tea from Mount Junshan also known as "Gold Inlaid Jade". This kind of tea was listed

后全部立于杯底，宛如刀枪林立，为茶中奇观。

洞庭湖湖畔的岳阳楼为千古名胜，自古有“洞庭天下水，岳阳天下楼”之称。它与武汉的黄鹤楼、南昌的滕王阁同为江南三大名楼。岳阳楼北依长江，南通湘江，遥对君山，极目望远，一碧无垠。相传这里在三国时曾是吴国将军鲁肃（172—217）训练水军的阅兵台，

as a tribute to the imperial family in the Tang Dynasty. The golden tea leaves narrow and thin as needles, are wrapped by a layer of white filaments. When the tea is being brewed, tea leaves first float up to the top and then sink to the bottom in a vertical position as if they were swords standing upward creating a peculiar phenomenon in the tea cup.

Yueyang Tower at the Dongting lakeside has always been a scenic attraction and eulogized since ancient

• 岳阳楼
Yueyang Tower

范仲淹

范仲淹，字希文,北宋名臣、政治家、军事家、文学家、思想家。范仲淹借《岳阳楼记》抒发了自己忧国忧民的政治情怀，其中的名句“先天下之忧而忧，后天下之乐而乐”流传千古。

Fan Zhongyan

Fan Zhongyan (989-1052) was a prominent official, politician, military strategist, thinker and literary figure of the Northern Song Dynasty. In his *Remarks of Yueyang Tower*, Fan expressed his feelings and concerns over his country and his people in the most quoted sentence through ages: "Bear the hardship and bitterness before others, enjoy comfort and happiness after others."

唐代扩建为楼阁。之后，著名诗人孟浩然、李白、杜甫、白居易等大文学家纷纷到此浏览，并留下许多诗赋名篇。宋代巴陵郡守滕子京重修岳阳楼，并嘱托范仲淹作《岳阳楼记》，从此，岳阳楼声名大振。岳阳楼高19.72米，宽17.2米，呈长

times as the first tower under heaven comparable to Dongting Lake as the first lake under heaven. It is one of the three famous towers south of the Yangtze River along with Huanghe (Yellow Crane) Tower of Wuhan and Tengwang Pavilion of Nanchang. One can enjoy a panoramic view of the lake from the tower with the Yangtze River to the north, Xiangjiang River in the south and Junshan Island in the front. According to legends, this location was once used as an inspection platform to review navy drills by Lu Su (172-217), a general of State Wu during the Three Kingdoms Period. It was expanded and built into the size of current Yueyang tower in the Tang Dynasty. Famous poets including Meng Haoran, Li Bai, Du Fu and Bai Juyi had all visited the tower leaving behind many well-known poems and literary works. In the Northern Song Dynasty, Baling County magistrate Teng Zijing rebuilt Yueyang Tower and requested the well-known literary master Fan Zhongyan to write about the tower. Fan's prose *Remarks of Yueyang Tower* won immense fame for the tower. The rectangular-shaped Yueyang Tower is 19.72 meters tall and 17.2 meters wide covering an area of 251 square meters. It

洞庭湖文化

据考古发现，洞庭湖的历史可以追溯到大约10万年以前的旧石器时代。这里保留了极为丰富的文化史迹，澧县鸡公垱旧石器遗址出土了石片、刮削器、石锤、石球、尖状器、砍砸器等200多件旧石器，从而证实了在10万多年前这里就有人类生存；洞庭湖区还发现了数十处新石器文化遗址，如汤家岗新石器时代遗址、三元宫新石器时代遗址、华容车轱山新石器时代遗址等。这些遗址都证明了洞庭湖区同样也是中华民族的文明发源地之一。

洞庭湖畔的古城岳阳有着悠久的历史，古称“巴陵”“岳州”，集名山、名水、名楼、名人、名文于一体，是湘楚文化的摇篮，也是中华灿烂历史文化的重要发祥地之一。

Dongting Culture

Based on archaeological findings, Dongting Lake's history can be traced back to the Paleolithic period about 100,000 years ago. Many historical sites of rich cultural heritage are well preserved in this area. The excavation at the Jigong Dang Paleolithic site in Lixian County found over 200 pieces of pre-historical stone tools including stone scrapers, stone hammers, stone balls and pointed stone choppers. This discovery has confirmed human existence in this area over 100,000 years ago. In addition, over a dozen of Neolithic cultural ruins were found in the Dongting Lake area including sites of Tangjia Gang, Sanyuan Gong and Chegu Shan of Hua Rong, all of which have proved that this area is one of the civilization cradles of the Chinese nationality.

The ancient city Yueyang by Dongting Lake has a long history known as "Baling" and "Yuezhou" in ancient times. The city is famous for its mountains, rivers, ancient buildings and noted literati. It is the cultural cradle of Sichuan and Hunan provinces and also one of the important birthplaces of the Chinese history and culture.

方形，占地251平方米，为四柱、三层、飞檐、盔顶、纯木建筑。楼顶陡而翘，层叠相衬，宛如古代士兵的头盔，故名“盔顶”，这在中国现存古建筑中是独一无二的。楼内各层挂满了历代名人的题咏，其中以李白的对联“水天一色，风月无边”最为著名。楼内藏有12块檀木板刻《岳阳楼记》全文，文章、书法、刻工、木料全属珍品，人称“四绝”。

滇池

滇池，古名“滇南泽”，位于云南省昆明市的西南部。滇池是由于地层断裂下陷而形成的构造湖泊。大约200万年前，滇池还是地壳上升区，后来受喜马拉雅山运动的影响，山地中间断裂下陷，盘龙江、柴河、梁王河等河流注入而成滇池。滇池南北向分布，湖体略呈弓形，湖面海拔1886.3米，湖面南北长39千米，东西宽13.5千米，湖岸线长199.5千米，面积290平方千米，是云贵高原最大的湖泊。

滇池孕育了灿烂的中国古代文化，其周围分布着多处新石器时代

is a wooden structure with four columns, three storeys, upturned eaves and a steep and raised roof top in the shape of an ancient soldier's helmet, a unique style unmatched in other extant ancient buildings in China. Inside the tower, walls on every floor are covered with literary works by famous writers and poets from different dynasties. The most famous ones are a couplet by Li Bai and Fan Zhongyan's *Remarks of Yueyang Tower* carved on 12 pieces of red sandalwood. The prose, the calligraphy, the carving techniques and the material used are all considered treasures known as "the Four Best".

Dianchi Lake

Dianchi Lake, known as "Diannan Marsh" in ancient times, is located in the southwest of Kunming City, Yunnan Province. Dianchi Lake is an ancient tectonic lake formed in the depression caused by fault movements. About 2 million years ago, rising earth crust in this area began to fault and sink due to tectonic movements in the Himalayas. Water from Panlong River, Chaihe River, Liangwang River and other rivers all flowed into the Dianchi basin and formed the lake. The bow-shaped Dianchi Lake

• 滇池风光
Scenery of Dianchi Lake

文化遗址，出土了大量陶片。据研究，部分陶片由谷穗或谷壳制作而成，表明此时滇池地区已经有了较为发达的原始农业。另外，出土的青铜器工艺品说明，在2000—2500年前，滇池地区的人民就已经可以在青铜器上雕镂、浇铸多种图像。

西山位于滇池西岸，海拔为

has an elevation of 1,886.3 meters. It is the largest lake on the Yunnan-Guizhou Plateau, 39 kilometers long from south to north and 13.5 kilometers wide from east to west covering an area of 298 square kilometers with a 199.5 kilometers long shoreline.

Splendid Chinese ancient culture was born around Dianchi Lake where large quantities of pottery pieces were unearthed in many Neolithic sites in the area. Potsherds were made of grain ears and chaffs, which demonstrates that primitive agriculture was already well developed in the arca around the lake in the Neolithic Age. Bronze crafts unearthed in this area also prove that people living around Dianchi Lake knew how to carve, cast and engrave portraits on bronze ware about 2,000 to 2,500 years ago.

Mount Xishan on the west shore of Dianchi Lake has an elevation of 2,511 meters. It is also known as Mount Sleeping Buddha because its shape resembles a sleeping Buddha. Viewed from the southeast of Kunming City, the distant Mount Xishan also appear to be a sleeping beauty, whose face, chest, abdomen, legs

- 纺织场面青铜贮贝器（西汉）

贮贝器的作用是盛放古滇国的货币——贝壳。贮贝器的器盖上采用分铸再焊接的技法，装饰了许多立体雕像，既有人物，也有动物，雕琢细腻，形象生动。

Bronze Money Box of Weaving Motif (Western Han Dynasty, 206 B.C.-25 A.D.)

The function of money boxes was to keep the money then. These boxes were beautifully made, very artistic, particularly their lids, often by welding cast parts together and having 3-D mini sculptures of human figures or animals, all being fine and vivid to make a roll of illustrations about history and culture.

2511米，因形似卧佛，所以又有“卧佛山”之名。自昆明城东南眺望，西山犹如一位酣睡的美女，脸、胸、腹、腿甚至垂入水中的头发都清晰可见，十分动人。“美人卧波”也因此成为名扬天下的美景。

龙门是云华洞和达天阁整个石凿工程的总称，是云南最大、最精美的道教石窟，始建于清代乾隆年间，历时73年开凿完成。这里所有的神像、香炉、台案都是就天然崖石镂空精雕而成，具有极高的欣赏价值。

滇池北岸的大观楼，建于清代康熙年间，为三层木结构建筑，也是观赏滇池美景的理想之地。自建

and even hair falling on the water can be seen clearly. This enchanting sight is known as "a Sleeping Beauty on Waves".

Yunhua Cave and Datian (Reach Heaven) Pavilion are the biggest and the most exquisite Taoist grottos in Yunnan Province, collectively called the Dragon Gate. Starting during Emperor Qianlong's reign, the construction took 73 years to complete. The statues of immortals with incent burners and tables inside the grottos are all hollow-out carvings with very high artistic values.

Daguan (Grand View) Tower is a three storey wooden structure built during Emperor Kangxi's reign of the Qing Dynasty. It is the best place to enjoy a panoramic view of Dianchi Lake. Since its completion, numerous poets and

• **龙门**（图片提供：全景正片）

龙门高出滇池水面300米，站在西山之巅俯瞰湖光山色，滇池美景可尽收眼底。

The Dragon Gate

The Dragon Gate on the top of the mountain is 300 meters above Dianchi Lake, providing a splendid scenic overlook of the lake and its surrounding areas.

• **大观楼**（图片提供：全景正片）
Daguan Tower

成之后，无数文人雅士登楼赋诗，清代诗人孙髯翁就在此地写下了古今第一长联，将滇池风景描绘得淋漓尽致。

洱海

洱海，古称“叶榆泽”，位于云南省西部的苍山东麓。洱海在第三纪喜马拉雅运动时形成断层陷落盆地，后汇集周围流水而形成构造湖。洱海南北长约40千米，东西平

writers visited the tower and left behind renowned literary works. Sun Ranweng, a poet in the Qing Dynasty, wrote the longest couplet here, giving the lake a thorough and vivid description.

Erhai Lake

Erhai Lake is located at the eastern foothills of Cangshan Mountain in the west of Yunnan Province, known as "Yeyu Marsh" in ancient times. Tertiary Himalayan movement caused water to

均宽约7—8千米，周长116千米，面积249平方千米，形如一弯新月，又因湖形似人耳，故名洱海。

自古以来，洱海一直被称做“群山间的无瑕美玉”。湖边的苍山高耸入云，19座山峰海拔都在3500米以上，终年白雪皑皑。洱海水清如玉，山水相映，有“玉洱银苍”之誉。“洱海月”是一大美景。

迄今为止，在洱海周围的山坡、台地上发现了30多处新石器时

flow into the fault basin and formed this tectonic lake. Erhai Lake is about 40 kilometers long from south to north and 7 to 8 kilometers wide on average from east to west covering an area of 249 square kilometers with a circumference of 116 kilometers. The lake has a shape resembling a crescent or a human ear, hence the name Erhai meaning Ear-shaped Sea.

Since ancient times, Erhai Lake has always been acclaimed as "the Flawless Jade in the Mountains". The towering

• 洱海风光
Scenery of Erhai Lake

• 白雪皑皑的点苍山
Snow-frosted Cangshan Mountain

代遗址，如海东金梭岛就是一个著名的新石器遗址，这里出土了大量石器、陶器、青铜器、铜柄铁刃剑等。由此可以推断这里或许就是古代白族先民冶炼、铸造青铜器的生产基地，因此也可以说，洱海就是白族的摇篮。

大理城的崇圣寺三塔面朝洱海，背靠苍山，呈三足鼎立之势，挺秀壮丽。主塔为千寻塔，高69.13米，为方形16层密檐式建筑，是中国古塔中偶数层数最多的塔。千寻塔建于南诏时期，塔顶有金属塔刹、宝盖、宝顶和金鸡等，塔前的照壁上刻有“永镇山川”四个大字，塔内垂直贯通上下，设有木质

Cangshan Mountain by the lake has 19 snowcapped peaks all above 3,500 meters in elevation. With the snowy mountain reflected on Erhai Lake's profound shade of aquamarine, the scenery is described as "jade-color, ear-shaped sea with a silver mountain". One of the most beautiful sights is "Moon over Erhai Lake".

More than 30 Neolithic sites have been discovered so far around Erhai Lake and in its surrounding hills and tableland. Jinsuo (Gold Shuttle) Island in the east of the lake is a famous Neolithic site where a large amount of stone tools, pottery, bronze and iron swords with copper handles were unearthed. These findings can be inferred that this place might be a production base for ancestors of the Bai ethnic group to smelt and cast bronze tools in ancient times. Therefore Erhai Lake can be considered the cradle of the Bai ethnic group.

The Chongsheng Temple in Dali City has a stunning ensemble of three independent pagodas arranged on the corners of an equilateral triangle, facing Erhai Lake and against Cangshan Mountain in the back. The main Qianxun Pagoda is a 69.13-meter high square-shaped structure of 16 storeys with each storey consisting of multiple tiers of

• 崇圣寺三塔
Three Pagodas in Chongsheng Temple

楼梯。元明时期，有不少文人登塔赋诗题字。千寻塔西约70米处，有南北两座小塔，各高42.19米，为八角形密檐式砖塔，塔身有佛像、莲花等浮雕。三塔布局统一，造型和谐，是南方最壮丽的塔群。三塔与远处的苍山、洱海相互辉映，使古城大理的自然人文风韵更加迷人。

upturned eaves. It has the most even-numbered floors among Chinese ancient pagodas. Built in the Nanzhao Period, Qianxun Pagoda has a metal top with a golden rooster sculpture and four big characters "*Yong Zhen Shan Chuan*" (meaning pacify the land forever) carved on the screen wall facing the gate of this pagoda. The inner wall of the pagoda is

hollow from the bottom to the top built with wooden stairs inside. During the Yuan and Ming dynasties, many scholars composed poems and inscriptions on the tower. Two sibling pagodas of 42.19 meters tall were built in the south and north about 70 meters west of Qianxun Pagoda. They are brick towers in an octagonal shape in an architectural design similar to the main pagoda. The pagoda walls are embossed with images of Buddha and lotus flowers. These three pagodas arranged in a unified and harmonious layout are the most magnificent pagoda ensemble in South China. The three pagoda ensemble, the distant Cangshan Mountain and Erhai Lake add more charm to the natural human landscape of the ancient city of Dali.

白族服饰

白族是中国少数民族之一，主要聚居于云南大理白族自治州。中国大陆约有187万白族人，其中云南有150多万。他们的服装极具民族特色。白族人民崇尚白色，男子一般头缠蓝色或白色包头，上身穿白色对襟衣，外套黑领褂，出门时还要背挂包，配长刀。女子多用绣花布或者彩色头巾缠头，穿白上衣、红坎肩，腰系绣花短围腰，手戴银或玉手镯，下穿蓝色长裤。女子头饰则有较大区别：未婚女子多梳独辫或将头发盘在花头巾之外，左侧垂下雪白的缨穗；已婚女子则在头顶挽发髻，用蓝色布帕包缠。

Costumes of Bai Ethnic Group

Bai ethnic group mainly lives in Dali Bai Autonomous Prefecture, Yunnan Province. In mainland China there are about 1.87 million Bai people of which over 1.5 million live in Yunnan Province. Their costumes have very distinctive features. As their name Bai (meaning white) suggests, the Bai people respect the color of white. Bai men usually wear a white jacket and a black vest with their heads wrapped in blue or white cloths at top. They carry a bag and a long sword when they go out. Bai women have headdresses made of embroidery or colorful cloths. Their outfit includes a white jacket topped with a red vest, an embroidered short apron tied at the waist, long blue pants and silver or jade bracelets. Most unmarried women wear a single pigtail or roll their hair up around a headdress on top with white strings hanging on the left side. Married women roll their hair up and covered with a blue-cloth headdress.

• 白族姑娘
A Bai Woman

泸沽湖

泸沽湖位于云南省宁蒗县与四川省盐源县交界处，海拔2609.7米，湖面面积48.45平方千米。此湖是因断层陷落而形成的高原湖泊，整个湖泊状若马蹄，东西窄而南北长，形如曲颈葫芦，故名“泸沽湖”。当地人称“谢纳咪”，意为大海、母湖。

泸沽湖由草海和亮海两部分组

Lugu Lake

Lugu Lake is located at the border between Yanyuan County of Sichuan Province and Ninglang County of Yunnan Province. It covers an area of 48.45 square kilometers with an elevation of 2609.7 meters. Lugu Lake is an alpine lake formed in a depression caused by fault movements. Shaped like a bottle gourd, it is narrower from east to west and longer from south to north, hence the

泸沽湖
Lugu Lake

• 里格岛
Lige Island in Lugu Lake

成。草海草木密实，透过晶莹的湖水，可以看到绿的、黄的和紫红色的水草。亮海如明镜一般透亮，波光粼粼，清明幽深。湖面颜色会随着日升日落而变化万千，黎明时分湖水被染成一片金红；太阳升起后湖面就会呈现翠绿色；黄昏太阳落山时湖水则会变成墨绿色。

泸沽湖内有5个小岛，湖的周围山峦起伏，西北面是格姆山，它状

name Lugu meaning bottle gourd. The local people call it "*Xienami*", meaning big sea or mother sea.

Lake Lugu has two distinctive features. One part of the lake is packed with dense vegetation, known as the "Grass Sea". Aquatic weeds in green, yellow and fuchsia colors can be easily seen through the clear water. The other part of the lake is as clear and translucent as a shining mirror. The color of the

如在湖边蹲伏休息的雄狮，惟妙惟肖，故也被称为“狮子山”。

lake changes dramatically following the sunrise and the sunset. At dawn, the lake is dyed golden red; the color changes to emerald green after sun-up; and the lake transforms to a dark green color at dusk when the sun sets.

Lugu Lake has five small islands surrounded by mountains. To the northwest of the lake stands the Mount Gemu, also known as Lion Mountain because the shape of the mountain resembles a lion resting at the lakeside.

• 摩梭姑娘
Mosuo Women

• 摩梭人的独木舟
A Mosuo Canoe

抚仙湖

抚仙湖位于云南省澄江、江川、华宁三县之间，因大部分水域在澄江县境内，故又名“澄江湖”。有两块大石耸立湖中，状如两位抚肩巡游的神仙，于是得名“抚仙石”，“抚仙湖”的名字也因此而来。

抚仙湖是由于地壳断裂下陷而形成的高原湖泊，湖面海拔1721

Fuxian Lake

Fuxian Lake is located between Chengjiang County, Jiangchuan County and Huaning County of Yunnan Province. As most of the lake is in Chengjiang County, it is also known as Chengjiang Lake. Standing in the middle of the lake are two huge rocks resembling two immortals touring the lake shoulder to shoulder, hence the name *Fuxian* meaning side-by-side immortals.

• 抚仙湖（图片提供：全景正片）
Fuxian Lake

米，湖区主要靠雨水供给。它北宽南窄，中部细长，形如倒放的葫芦，面积约211平方千米，平均水深87米，最深处达155米，是中国著名的深水湖泊。

抚仙湖湖水清澈透明，透明度有时可达7—8米，中国明代地理学家徐霞客曾记述“唯抚仙湖最清”。湖西南处有一座小岛，名“大孤山”，形状似鸡蛋，面积约0.5平方千米。据史料记载，明代时，有许多文人名士在此岛兴建亭台楼阁，使它成为抚仙湖一大胜景。湖西面的尖山平地而起，犹如玉笋一般直插云霄，被称为“玉笋擎天”。

在抚仙湖南面还存在一种奇怪的现象，星云湖与抚仙湖通过海门河而通，可是，两湖的鱼却互不来往。河中段树立着一块“界鱼石”，据说两湖的鱼到此便立刻掉头回游。其原因有可能与两湖的水质、水温不同有关。由于抚仙湖水深风大，湖中很少有生物存活。但湖中有一种鱼，因其能在风大浪高的湖中生存，当地人民称其为“抗浪鱼”。此鱼刺软、

It is an alpine lake formed in the depression caused by tectonic movements. The lake is at 1,721 meters in elevation and mainly fed by rain. It is shaped like a gourd placed upside down, wider in the north and narrower in the south with a slender middle section. It is a famous deep lake in China covering an area of 211 square kilometers with an average depth of 87 meters and the maximum depth of 155 meters.

The water in Fuxian Lake is crystal-clear with a transparency of up to 7-8 meters. The Ming Dynasty geographer Xu Xiake once commended the lake as the clearest of all lakes. In the southwest of the lake, there is an egg-shaped islet of 0.5 square kilometers called Mount Dagu, which was visited by many noted poets and writers during the Ming Dynasty according to historical records. Their visits promoted constructions of pavilions and pagodas on the islet, making it one of the best scenic attractions on Fuxian Lake. To the west of the lake, a mountain rises abruptly from the ground as if a bamboo shoot made of jade pierced the sky. This scenery is described as "Jade Bamboo Shoot Supporting the Heaven".

• 大孤山（图片提供：全景正片）
Mount Dagu

肉细、味美，因在清代被列为朝廷贡品而闻名于世。

纳木错

纳木错位于西藏自治区拉萨市当雄、班戈两县之间，“纳木错”为藏语，蒙古语又称“腾格里海”“腾格里湖”，都是“天湖”之意。几百万年以前，地壳运

A strange phenomenon exists in the south of the lake where Fuxian Lake and Xingyun (Star Cloud) Lake merge into Haimen (Sea Gate) River. But the fish in one lake never mingles with the fish from the other lake. It is said that the fish from both lakes would turn back when they hit a fishing boundary stone erected in the middle of Haimen River. The real reason might lie in the difference of water quality and temperature between the two lakes. Fuxian Lake is known to have deep water and strong wind, which make it difficult for many species to survive, except for one type of ray-finned fish. The local people call it "Kanglang fish" meaning fish resistant to waves. The fish was listed as a tribute to the imperial family in the Qing Dynasty because of its soft bones, fine meat and delicious taste.

Namtso

Namtso (Nam Co or Lake Namu) is situated between Damxung County of Lhasa Prefecture and Baingoin County of Nagqu Prefecture in the Xizang Autonomous Region. It is also called "Tengri Nor" meaning "the heavenly lake". Several million years ago, violent crustal movements happened here. Some locations rose up and became plateaus,

动使岩层受到严重挤压，有的褶皱隆起成为高山，有的凹陷下落成为谷地或山间盆地。纳木错就是在地壳陷落的基础上，受冰川作用影响而形成的。湖水来源主要是天然降水和高山冰雪融水，湖水不外流，是西藏第一大内陆湖。湖形狭长，东西长70千米，南北宽30千米，面积1940平方千米。纳木

and some sank and became valleys and basins. Namtso formed in a tectonic basin as a result of glaciation impact. Namtso is the largest endorheic lake in Xizang and its water mainly comes from natural rainfall and melted mountain snow. It is long and narrow, 70 kilometers from east to west and 30 kilometers from south to north covering an area of 1,940 square kilometers. At 4,718 meters in

纳木错湖边的玛尼堆（图片提供：全景正片）

玛尼堆广泛分布在西藏各地的山间、路口、湖边、江畔，每逢佳节良辰，人们就会往上添加石子，用额头碰触，并虔诚祈祷。

Mani Stone Mounds on Namtso Lakeside

Mani stones are placed together along mountain trails, roadsides, riversides and lakeside all over Tibet. During holidays people add more stones to them or touch their foreheads on the stones as a gesture of devout praying.

错湖面海拔4718米，因此也是世界上海拔最高、面积超过1000平方千米的大湖。

纳木错是藏族人心目中的圣湖。湖中分布着三个岛屿，其中最大的是良多岛。另外还有五个半岛从不同的方位凸入水域，千姿百态的石林、溶洞以及天生桥等遍布半岛。其中扎西半岛居五个半岛之冠。“扎西”是藏语“吉祥”的意思，扎西半岛也被称做“吉祥爱情

elevation, Namtso is the highest lake above the sea level among lakes of more than 1,000 square kilometers.

Namtso is regarded as a sacred lake by Tibetans. There are three islands of which Kuhi Ne Drubphuk (Liangduo Island) is the largest. A variety of stone forests, karst caves and natural bridges are distributed in another five peninsulas protruding into the lake from different locations. Located in the southeast of the lake, the fist-shaped Tashi Dor of 10

• **纳木错湖边的合掌石**（图片提供：FOTOE）
Rocks of Closed Palms on Namtso Lakeside

• 扎西半岛上的白塔（图片提供：FOTOE）
White Pagoda on the Tashi Dor

岛”。扎西半岛位于湖的东南侧，远远望去，犹如一只伸入湖中的拳头，面积约10平方千米。半岛上最引人注目的就是两个高大挺拔的石柱，好像两只手掌在拍手欢迎来客，又像一对肩并肩的情侣，所以有“合掌石”“情侣石”之称。

湖的四面建有4座寺庙，其中位于湖西岸的多加寺规模最大，佛殿建在崖洞中，殿前有一座白塔，很是醒目。多加寺高踞悬崖之上，三面环湖，正对念青唐古拉山脉，是观看湖光山色的好地方。

square kilometers is considered the best of the five peninsulas. Tashi means lucky in Tibetan, therefore Tashi Dor is also called "an island of love and luck". The most striking attractions on Tashi Dor are the two huge stone columns known as "Rocks of Closed Palms" or "Rocks of Lovers" because of their resemblance of two lovebirds or two hands clapping to welcome visitors.

There are four monasteries around the lake. The largest one is Droja Temple in the west bank of the lake, built in a cliff cave with a striking white pagoda in the front. Standing on top of a precipice and facing Nyainqentanglha mountain range and water on three sides, Droja Temple is considered one of the best locations to view Namtso Lake and its surrounding mountains.

扎陵湖和鄂陵湖

扎陵湖和鄂陵湖位于青藏高原巴颜喀拉山北麓，是因局部地壳下陷而形成的构造湖。两湖相距约20千米，形似蝴蝶，是黄河源头地区两个最大的高原淡水湖泊，也是黄河源头地区众水汇聚之地，有“双生湖”“黄河源头姊妹湖”之称。黄河发源于青藏高原巴颜喀拉山，

Gyaring Lake and Ngoring Lake

Gyaring Lake and Ngoring Lake are tectonic lakes at the northern foot of the Bayan Har Mountain Range on the Qinghai-Tibetan Plateau. Twenty kilometers apart and shaped like a butterfly, these lakes are the two largest freshwater lakes on the plateau and the source of the Yellow River where all the watercourses converge. They are known

• 扎陵湖（图片提供：全景正片）
Gyaring Lake

流经星宿海和玛曲河(又名孔雀河)，首先注入扎陵湖，然后经过一条很宽的河谷再流入鄂陵湖。

扎陵湖位于青海省果洛藏族自治州的玛多县，形如贝壳，又叫“查灵海”。扎陵湖是黄河源区第二大淡水湖，南北长约35千米，东西宽约21.6千米，面积达526平方千米。湖水一半清澈，一半发白，因此又有“白色长湖”之称。扎陵湖的西南部有三个小岛，岛上岩石嶙峋，栖息着鱼鸥、赤麻鸭、黑颈鹤等多种候鸟，当地人们称这些小岛为“青海的第二鸟岛”。据说，唐朝文成公主嫁往西藏，松赞干布曾在扎陵湖周围设帐扎寨，迎候文成公主的到来，并在湖畔完成了婚礼仪式。

鄂陵湖位于扎陵湖以东，在青海玉树藏族自治州的曲麻莱县境内，形如金钟，又称“鄂灵海”。鄂陵湖是黄河源区第一大淡水湖，南北长约32.3千米，东西宽约31.6千米，湖面面积610平方千米。湖水颜色极为清澈，呈深绿色，故有“蓝色长湖”之称。

扎陵湖和鄂陵湖区有着丰富的鱼类资源，湖中大多为冷水性无鳞

as "the twin lakes" or "the sister lakes at the source of the Yellow River". The Yellow River starts from Bayan Har Mountain, passes through Xingxiuhai River and Maqu River (or Peacock River), and flows into Gyaring Lake first and then into Ngoring Lake through a very wide river valley.

Gyaring Lake (or Zhaling Sea) is located in Madoi County of Golog Tibet Autonomous Prefecture in Qinghai Province. The shell-shaped lake is the second largest freshwater lake in the Yellow River source area. It is 35 kilometers long from south to north and 21.6 kilometers wide from east to west covering 526 square kilometers. The water in the lake is half clear and half white, hence the name "the white long lake". In the southwest of the lake, there are three islets inhabited by a variety of migratory birds on steep rocks including great black-headed gulls, ruddy shelducks and black-necked cranes. Local people call these three islets "the second largest bird island in Qinghai". According to legends, King Songtsen Gampo of Tubo set up tents at the Gyaring lakeside to greet Princess Wen -cheng of the Tang Dynasty and completed their wedding ceremony here.

鱼，如花斑裸鲤、骨唇黄河鱼、三眼鱼等。过去生活在这里的藏民有敬鱼的习俗，从不捕鱼、吃鱼，所以湖中的鱼类得以自然繁殖。

• 湖畔的经幡（图片提供：全景正片）

Sutra Streamer on the Lakeside

Ngoring Lake (or Ngoring Sea) is located to the east of the Gyaring Lake in the Qumarlêb County of Yushu Tibetan Autonomous Prefecture, Qinghai Province. The bell-shaped lake is the largest freshwater lake in the Yellow River source area with a north-south extent of 32.3 kilometers and an east-west extent of 31.6 kilometers covering an area of 610 square kilometers. The extremely clear water in the lake displays a dark blue color, hence the name "the blue long lake".

Both Gyaring Lake and Ngoring Lake have abundant fish stocks, most of which are cold-water species without scale such as Chuanchia labiosa, Huanghe naked carps and three-eyed fish. Tibetans living in this area before had a custom of respecting fish, so they never caught or ate fish. This tradition enabled the uninhibited natural reproduction of fish in the lake.

文成公主进藏

吐蕃王朝是中国西藏历史上有明确史料记载的政权。629年，松赞干布即位赞普，经过3年征战，使吐蕃王朝恢复统一。松赞干布富于政治远见，积极与唐王朝建立友好关系。唐贞观十四年（640年），松赞干布派使者携带黄金、珠宝等来唐朝请婚。第二年，文成公主带领一些精通纺织、建筑、造纸、酿酒、制陶、冶金、农具制造等先进生产技术的工匠，以及佛经、历法、医药、种子等自长安前往吐蕃和亲。入藏后，跟随文成公主的工匠教当地的藏族同胞灌溉、除草、施肥，并将种桑养蚕的技术传授给他们，使吐蕃人的生活水平得到了很大的提高。此外，文成公主入藏后，建寺弘佛，修建了小昭寺，促进了佛教在吐蕃的盛行。总的来说，汉藏联姻对西藏经济、文化等方面的发展，起到了积极的作用。同时，有力地促进了汉藏和谐，民族团结。

- 西藏大昭寺内描绘文成公主进吐蕃的壁画

A Mural Painting in Jokhang Temple, Xizang, Depicting a Scene When Princess Wencheng Was Welcomed in Tubo (Ancient Tibet)

Princess Wencheng

The Tubo Kingdom is a regime with clear historical records in the history of Xizang, China. In the year 629, Songtsen Gampo became the king of Tubo and unified Tubo after three years of crusade. He was a man of political vision actively promoting friendly relationship with the Tang Dynasty. In 640 Songtsen Gampo sent an ambassador together with gold and jewelry to Tang requesting a marriage. The second year Princess Wencheng traveled to Tubo to complete the wedding and brought with her advanced technology in textile, construction, paper making, winemaking, pottery, metallurgy and agricultural tool-making techniques as well as Buddhist sutra, calendar, medicine and seeds. After her arrival in Xizang, craftsmen who came with the princess taught the local Tibetans irrigation, weeding, fertilizing, and sericulture techniques. As a result, the living standard of the local people was greatly improved. Moreover, her coming to Xizang helped to build the Ramoche Temple and promote the spread of Buddhism in Tubo. In general, this Tibetan-Han marriage had a positive impact in the development of Tibetan economy and culture. Meanwhile, Han people also learned a lot about Tibetan culture and their experience in Xizang in turn improved the harmony and unity between Tibetans and Han people.

青海湖

青海湖古称“西海”，从北魏（386—534）开始，才更名为“青海”。青海湖位于青海省东北部，湖面海拔为3193.92米，东西长106千米，南北宽63千米，周长360千米，面积4635平方千米，是中国海拔最高、面积最大的内陆湖泊和咸水湖。200 万年前，剧烈的造山运动使青藏高原周围形成了大大小小的湖泊，青海湖就是其中的一个巨大湖泊。当时，青海湖周围有100 多条河

Qinghai Lake

Qinghai Lake (or Koko Nur) used to be called *Xihai* (West Sea) and had the name changed to Qinghai (Blue Sea) after the North Wei Dynasty (386-534). Located in the northeast of Qinghai Province, the lake is the highest and largest endorheic lake and saltwater lake in China. It is 106 kilometers long from east to west and 63 kilometers wide from south to north covering a total of 4,635 square kilometers with a circumference of 360 kilometers and an altitude of 3193.92 meters. About 2 million years ago, many

流注入湖中，同时湖水又从东面输往黄河。大约在100万年前，湖东面的日月山发生了强烈隆起，堵住了青海湖的出口，使青海湖成为一个闭塞湖。

湖中分布着鸟岛、海心山、海西山、沙岛、三块石等五座小岛。其中，海西山（又名小西山）和鸟岛（蛋岛）候鸟最为集中，一眼望去，全是密密麻麻的鸟巢。每年的五六月份，是青海湖观鸟的最佳时节，现在，这两个小岛已被列入国

big and small lakes came into being around the Qinghai-Tibet Plateau as a result of intense orogenic movements. Qinghai Lake was one of the largest lakes. During that time, over 100 rivers flowed into Qinghai Lake, which in turn fed the Yellow River from the east side. About 1 million years ago, Riyue (Sun and Moon) Mountain to the east of the lake rose substantially and blocked the outlet of the water making it an isolated lake with only inflow and no outflow.

Distributed in the lake are five small

• 青海湖
Qinghai Lake

家重点自然保护区。

海心山位于湖中心略偏南，早在汉代，岛上就建立了寺庙、白塔。海心山上还有一座古城——应龙城，唐朝将领哥舒翰曾在岛上建城练兵。

青海湖一带是重要的畜牧业产地，尤其养马业比较发达。早在春秋战国时期，这一带的“秦马”就以雄壮、善驰而闻名。隋唐时，这里的“秦马”“乌孙马”“汗血马”就以能征善战而著称。唐朝时，朝廷在青海设置有茶马司，进行专门的茶叶与马匹的交易。

• 鸟岛（图片提供：全景正片）
Bird Island

islands: the Bird Island, Mount Haixin (the Heart of the Lake) Island, Mount Haixi (West of Sea) Island, Sha (Sand) Island and Three-Rock Island. Mount Haixi Island (or Small Western Mountain Island) and the Bird Island (or Egg Island) have the most migratory birds in crowded nests. Today, these two islands have been listed as the key national nature reserves. The best bird-watching season at Qinghai Lake is between May and June.

Mount Haixin Island in the south of the lake center has a temple and a white pagoda built in the Han Dynasty. On Mount Haixin stands an ancient city called Yinglong Town built by Ge Shuhan, a Tang Dynasty general, who stationed his army here.

The Qinghai Lake area has always been an important place for animal husbandry, especially in horse breeding. As early as the Spring and Autumn and Warring States periods, horses such as "Qin horses" reared in this region were famous for their strength and outstanding gallop. "Wusun horses" and "Hanxue (Blood Sweat) horses" were also well-known for their ability in battles during the Sui and Tang dynasties. The Tang imperial court set up a department in

• **青海湖畔的牧场**
Lakeside Ranch at Qinghai Lake

博斯腾湖

博斯腾湖又名“巴格拉什湖”，位于新疆维吾尔自治区天山支脉库鲁克山南麓，塔克拉玛干大沙漠北部边缘的焉耆盆地内。塔里木盆地西部的开都河，以及盆地北坡诸河汇集而形成了博斯腾湖。博斯腾湖古称“西海”，唐代称“鱼海”，清代始称“博斯腾湖”。湖区略呈三角形，东西长55千米，南北宽25千米，湖水最深处达16.5米，

Qinghai specifically to conduct trading between tea and horses.

Bosten Lake

Bosten Lake is situated in the Yanqi Basin on the northern border of Taklimakan Desert and the southern foot of the Kuruktag Range of Tianshan (Heavenly) Mountains in Xinjiang Uyghur Autonomous Region. The lake is fed by Kaidu River to the west of Tarim Basin and a catchment of various tributaries north of the Tarim Basin.

博斯腾湖（图片提供：FOTOE）
Bosten Lake

面积1019平方千米，是中国最大的内陆淡水湖。

湖的北岸有一座人工沙岛，名叫“天格尔岛”，岛面积约11平方千米。湖岸分布有许多沙堤，将湖湾拦截成潟湖，这是受西北风和东北风影响而形成的。

湖分大小湖区，大湖水域辽阔，被誉为沙漠瀚海中的一颗明珠；大湖西侧的小湖形似珠链，芦苇丛生，芦苇沼泽面积达350多平方千米，是中国最大的芦苇荡。在

Bosten Lake was called "West Sea" in ancient times, "Sea of Fish" in the Tang Dynasty and the mane Bosten originated in the Qing Dynasty. The triangle-shaped lake is 55 kilometers long from east to west and 25 kilometers wide from south to north covering an area of 1,019 square kilometers with a depth up to 16.5 meters. It is the largest inland freshwater lake in China.

On the northern shore of the lake there is a manmade sand island called Tengri Island in an area of 11 square

金秋季节，金黄色的苇叶与雪白的芦花交相辉映，蔚为壮观。

博斯腾湖区是新疆最大的渔业生产基地，湖中鱼种繁多，如新疆大头鱼、草鱼、五道黑等，其中以鲤鱼和鲫鱼最多。由于湖区没有水污染，各类鱼都体大味美。

博斯腾湖被当地人称为“母亲湖”，每年的6月15日，蒙古族男女老少都会身着盛装前来参加盛大

• 金秋季节的芦苇荡（图片提供：FOTOE）
Reed Marsh in Golden Autumn

kilometers. Strong wind from northwest and northeast brought about many sand dykes which are distributed along the lakeshore. These embankments blocked water from the bay and contributed to formation of many lagoons.

Bosten Lake is divided into large and small lake areas. The large open area is known as the shining jewel in the sea of deserts. The smaller lakes to the west of the large area are connected with each other in a reed marshland of over 350 square kilometers, the largest reed marsh in China. In the golden season of autumn, the reed marsh displays a magnificent sight of golden reed leaves illuminated with white reed flowers.

Bosten Lake is the largest fishery production base and abundant in many fish species particularly carps such as crucian, bullhead and grass carps as well as river perch. The lake produces tasty fish thanks to unpolluted water resources.

The local people call Bosten Lake "Mother Lake". Every year on June 15th, Mongolian men, women and children are all dressed up to participate in a grand and sacred sacrifice ceremony for the lake. A sacrifice boat is decorated with flowers, flags and ribbons in blue, red, white, green and yellow colors implying

而又神圣的祭湖仪式。人们要将祭湖船上挂满蓝、红、白、绿、黄五种颜色的彩带，寓意“国泰民安、避邪避难、健康长寿、多子多孙、前程似锦”。同时，还要插满各种彩旗和花朵，船舱里盛满用炒面捏制的马、牛等动物造型以及水果、糕点、糖果等，船中间还要放置祭祀湖神用的金银铜币、珍珠玛瑙、五谷杂粮等。然后，蒙古族小伙子将祭湖船扛到祭湖台，长者大声念诵祝赞词，蒙古族女子唱蒙古长调《祭湖歌》。最后人们将祭湖船放入湖中，任其飘向远方。仪式结束后，人们便可以尽情品尝美食。

赛里木湖

赛里木湖，古称“净海”，位于新疆维吾尔自治区博尔塔拉蒙古自治州博乐市境内。大约在7000万年前，喜马拉雅造山运动使群峰崛起，围造出这个巨大的湖泊。由于周围山地有很多石灰岩裸露，湖中溶入大量的碳酸钙，从而让湖水更加清澈纯净。赛里木，是哈萨克语，意为“祝愿”，湖的东西长约30千米，南北宽约25千米，面积为

stability, peace, avoidance of evils and disasters, longevity, many descendants and a bright future. Inside the boat is filled with horses and cows made of fried dough as well as fruits, candies and pastries. Additionally gold and silver coins, pearls and agates, and grains and cereals are placed in the middle of the boat as offerings to the god of lake. Young Mongolian men carry the boat to a ceremonial platform. The elderly reads the sutra loudly accompanied by *Lake Ritual Song* sung by Mongolian women. Finally the boat is placed onto the lake and let go. After this ceremony, people start to enjoy wine and food.

Sayram Lake

Sayram Lake is located in Bole City of Bortala Mongolian Autonomous Prefecture, Xinjiang Uygurs Autonomous Region. It was known as "sea of purity" in ancient times. About 70 million years ago, the Himalayan orogenic movement caused rising of many peaks and created this huge lake surrounded by mountain ranges. A large amount of calcium carbonate from the nearby bare limestone mountains dissolved in the lake making the water much cleaner and

453平方千米，湖略呈卵圆形。又因这里是大西洋暖湿气流最后到达的地方，所以赛里木湖被称做“大西洋的最后一滴眼泪”。

“净海七彩”是赛里木湖水景的典型代表。赛里木湖湖水很深，透明度高。由于水底地形、波浪潮涌以及天空状况等原因，湖水色彩

clearer. "Sayram" means "blessing" in the Kazakh language. The oval-shaped lake covers 453 square kilometers, 20 kilometers long from east to west and 25 kilometers wide from south to north. The lake is also known as the "last teardrop of the Atlantic Ocean", as it is the last place reached by the Atlantic warm and humid air.

• 赛里木湖（图片提供：全景正片）
Sayram Lake

斑斓，赤、橙、黄、绿、青、蓝、紫等颜色一应俱全。湖边景物倒映在水中，清晰逼真，也被染上五彩的颜色。

历史上这里是丝绸之路天山北道的必经之地，湖区文化底蕴深厚，有许多寺庙遗址、岩画、碑刻以及古驿站遗址等。湖南岸的靖海寺和湖中小岛上的龙王庙就是人们为了祈求平安而建造的。果子沟位于赛里木湖南侧，是中国通往中亚、欧洲的咽喉要道，有“铁关”之称。元代和清代，政府都曾在沟内设置驿站，为过往的官兵、商旅

• 那达慕大会上的赛马（图片提供：FOTOE）
Horse Racing in Naadam Festival

The description "seven colors in the Sea of Purity" represents typical scenery of Sayram Lake, which has considerable depth and a high level of water transparency. The lake displays a wide range of colors in red, orange, yellow, green, cyan, blue and purple depending on the changes in tides, climate and underwater terrains. The reflection of the lakeside landscape in the water is also painted with various colors.

In history, the Silk Road travelers must pass this location if they took the northern routes of Tianshan Mountains. The areas around the lake have deep cultural traditions with many ancient temple and caravansary ruins, rock paintings and inscriptions. The Jinghai Temple on the southern shore and the Dragon King Temple on an island in the lake were built to pray for peace and stability. The Guozi (fruits) Valley to the south of the lake used to be a key thoroughfare, known as the "iron checkpoint" to Central Asia and Europe from China. Both Yuan and Qing dynasties set up caravansaries here to provide food and supplies for soldiers and traveling traders. Emperor Qianlong of the Qing Dynasty ordered to build two commanding caravansaries responsible

提供饮食，方便来往商客。清代乾隆皇帝平定准噶尔叛乱后在果子沟设立了头台、二台两座驿站，专门负责传递朝廷政令和边防军情。

每年七八月间，赛里木湖周围的蒙古族牧民都要举行盛大的那达慕大会。“那达慕”，在蒙古语中意为“娱乐”“游戏”。四面八方的蒙古族牧民身穿盛装，相约而至，欢庆丰收，载歌载舞，举行具有浓郁民族特色的赛马、叼羊、摔跤、姑娘追、阿肯弹唱等体育、文娱活动。

for delivering the court decree and battle status on the border to the court after he defeated the Junggar rebellion.

Every year in July and August, Mongolians living around the lake gather together in colorful costumes for the grand Naadam festival to celebrate harvests. Naadam means "games" in Mongolian. There are all kinds of popular ethnic activities and competitions featuring general horse racing, sheep catching on the horse, wrestling, and girl chasing games as well as dancing and singing.

丝绸之路

丝绸之路，是指西汉（前206—公元25）时，张骞出使西域开辟的以长安（今西安）为起点，经甘肃、新疆，到中亚、西亚，并联结地中海各国的陆上通道。通过这条漫漫长路运送的货物中，以中国的丝绸最具代表性，因此得名“丝绸之路”。通过这条贯穿欧亚的大道，中国的丝、绸、绫、缎、绢等丝制品，源源不断地运向中亚和欧洲，中亚等地的珠宝、香料、皮货、药材等也大批量地传入中国。丝绸之路促进了亚欧各国和中国的经济文化交流。

Silk Road

Silk Road refers to a historical network of interlinking trade routes opened up during the West Han Dynasty (206B.C. 25 A.D.) by the imperial envoy Zhang Qian to the west of China. Starting from Xi'an the routes across Gansu and Xinjiang connected to Mediterranean countries through Central and West Asia. The Silk Road got its name from the lucrative Chinese silk trade which provided a steady flow of products made of various Chinese silk fabrics. In turn large quantities of jewelry, spices, leather goods and herbs were brought back to China. The Silk Road promoted economic and cultural exchanges between China and other Asian countries and European countries.

- 张骞出使西域壁画
Mural Describing the Trip to the West by the Imperial Envoy Zhang Qian

日月潭

日月潭是台湾省最大的天然湖泊，旧称“水沙连”“水社大湖”，位于台湾省中部的南投县鱼池乡水社村。日月潭是由于局部地层陷落而形成的构造湖，面积7.73平方千米，周长35千米。最初，日月潭是两个单独的湖泊，在日本侵略者占据台湾时，为了发电的需要，

Sun-Moon Lake

Sun-Moon Lake (*Riyue Tan*) is the largest natural lake in Taiwan Province, known as "water-sand joint" and "the big lake of Shuishe" in the old days. It is located in Shuishe Village of Yuchi Town in Nantou County, central Taiwan Province, covering 7.73 square kilometers with a 35-kilometer circumference. It is a tectonic lake formed by partial depression

在下游筑坝，导致水位上升，淹没众多小山丘，两湖就连为一体形成了今天的日月潭。潭中有一小岛名珠子屿（光华岛），似浮在水面上的一颗明珠。以此岛为界，北半湖形状如大大的太阳，南半湖形状如弯弯的月亮，日月潭因此而得名。

of the earth. Originally there were two independent lakes. After the Japanese occupied Taiwan Province, dams were built for hydroelectric power plants at the lake's downstream causing the water level to rise and eventually submerge many small hills. As a result, the two lakes merged into today's Sun-Moon Lake. The lake is divided by a small island called

• **日月潭**（图片提供：全景正片）
Sun-Moon Lake

日月潭湖面辽阔，湖水澄澈。潭东的水社大山高2000多米，重峦叠嶂。南面的青龙山，地势险峻，巍峨挺拔。潭的四周分布着许多寺庙和古塔，如文武庙、玄奘寺和慈恩塔。文武庙建于1932年，位于日月潭北面山腰上，因祭祀孔子、关羽而得名。庙前有石阶365级，俗称“走一年”。正门为墨绿色大理石牌坊，拾阶而上，一对枣红色巨型狮子格外醒目。庙宇以金黄色为主，前殿为拜殿，主要作祭祀之用，为楼阁式建筑。正殿主要祭祀关羽，位居全庙正中，为正方形殿堂，名“武圣殿”。后殿主要祭祀孔子，为重檐庑殿式建筑，名“大成殿”。

玄奘寺位于潭南青龙山麓，是专门为纪念唐代玄奘法师而建的寺院，为仿唐式建筑，1965年建成。玄奘寺共有三层，第一层正殿的门楣上有“玄奘殿”三个大字。殿内供奉玄奘法师负笈像；第二层是供奉玄奘法师佛位的主殿；第三层有塔，名“玄奘宝塔”，用来供奉玄奘的舍利子，同时存放着玄奘的经典著作。

Jade Island (or Guanghua Island) into two parts. The northern part has a shape of a big sun and the southern part resembles a crescent moon, hence the name Sun-Moon Lake.

This large lake with crystal-clear water is surrounded by magnificent and precipitous mountains including Mount Shuishe at over 2,000 meters in elevation to the east and Mount Qinglong (Black Dragon) to the south along with many ancient temples and pagodas, such as Wenwu Temple, Xuanzang Temple and Ci'en Pagoda. Located in the northern hillside, Wenwu Temple (Temple of Cultural and Martial Gods) was built in 1932 to worship Confucius and Guan Yu. It has 365 stairs known as "a year of walk". Right in the front stands a big dark green marble archway, which leads to two huge striking vermillion lions a few steps up. The entire temple structure is painted mainly in golden-yellow color. The pavilion-style front hall is mainly used for worship ceremonies; the square-shaped main hall in the center of the temple is the God of War Hall dedicated to Guan Yu; and the rear hall with upturned double eaves is the Grand Achievement Hall dedicated to Confucius.

• 日月潭边的文武庙（图片提供：全景正片）

Wenwu Temple beside the Sun-Moon Lake

慈恩塔是仿辽宋古塔式样的八角宝塔。塔前绿茵遍地，花木繁茂，环境相当清幽。慈恩塔建在海拔955米的青龙山山顶，塔九层，高约45米，是日月潭景区的最高点。站在塔顶，可将日月潭美景尽收眼底。

Xuanzang Temple at the foot of Mount Qinglong south of the lake was completed in 1965 in memory of Buddhist Monk Xuanzang of the Tang Dynasty, which is modeled after a Tang-style building. The first floor of the temple has three big characters of "*Xuan Zang Dian*" (Xuanzang Hall) hanging on the door lintel and a statue of Monk Xuanzang on his way to seek knowledge; the second floor, considered the main floor, contains Monk Xuanzang's shrine; and the pagoda that keeps Xuanzang's Buddhist relic and many of his classic works is at the third floor.

Ci'en Pagoda was modeled after ancient octagonal pagodas from the Liao and Song dynasties. The 45-meter tall pagoda has nine storeys and is located in a quiet and secluded area with lush green plants and trees at the top of Mount Qinglong, 955 meters in elevation. It is the highest spot of all Sun-Moon Lake attractions. When standing at the top of the pagoda, one can enjoy a birds-eye view of the entire lake.

> 火山口湖

长白山天池

长白山天池，又称“白头山天池”“龙潭”，坐落在吉林省东南部，是中国和朝鲜的界湖，也是松花江、图们江、鸭绿江三江的源头。长白山天池的形成与火山活动有密切的关系。大约在6亿年前，这里还是一片汪洋大海。后来，一系列的造山运动使海水退走，长白山地区的地壳发生抬升、断裂，地下的岩浆也沿着地壳裂缝喷出地面，形成了以天池为中心的巨大火山锥。

火山喷发停止后，火山口逐渐潴水成湖。天池主要靠雨水、雪水以及地下泉水来供应。天池略呈椭圆形，面积约9.8平方千米，周长约13千米，南北长4.85千米，东西宽

> Crater Lakes

Heavenly Lake (*Tianchi*) of Changbai Mountains

Heavenly Lake (*Tianchi*) at the top of Changbai Mountais (Perpetually White Mountains) is located in the southeast of Jilin Province on the border between China and Korea, also known as "the Heavenly Lake on the White-headed Mountains" or "the Dragon Lake". It is the source of Songhua River (Sunggari River), Tumen River and Yalu River. The formation of Heavenly Lake was caused by volcanic activities. About 600 million years ago, this region was a vast ocean. Later a series of orogenic movements made the ocean water recede and underground magma gushed out to the ground from the cracks by crustal uplift, which formed a huge volcanic cone with today's Heavenly Lake as the center.

After the eruption, a lake formed

• **长白山天池**（图片提供：全景正片）
Heavenly Lake of Changbai Mountains

3.35千米，湖水最深处达373米，是中国最大的火山口湖，也是中国最深的湖泊。其海拔高达2194米，故取名为"天池"，是中国海拔最高的火山口湖。

长白山因其主峰白头山多白色浮石与积雪而得名。天池被长白山巍峨陡峻的16峰环抱。湖水由天池北面的湖口流入，然后从70多米的悬崖峭壁上倾斜而下，形成了著名的长白山瀑布。长白山瀑布是

as water accumulated in the volcanic crater. Heavenly Lake is mainly fed by rain, melted snow and underground spring water. The oval-shaped lake is 4.85 kilometers long from south to north and 3.35 kilometers wide from east to west covering an area of 9.8 square kilometers with a circumference of about 13 kilometers and a maximum depth of 373 meters. It is the deepest lake and the largest crater lake in China. Of all the crater lakes in China it has the highest

• 长白山瀑布（图片提供：全景正片）
Changbai Mountains Waterfall

世界落差最大的火山湖瀑布，坡陡水急，远远望去犹如一架斜立的天梯，因此有"通天河"之称。瀑布水流长年不断，一泄千丈，数里之外都能听到轰鸣的水声。

长白山地区天气严寒，气候多变，使天池湖水变化无常。有时上午天气晴好，风和日丽，湖面平静；下午便会狂风呼啸，甚至暴雨倾盆，池中惊涛骇浪，动人心魄。

elevation of 2,194 meters, hence the name "Heavenly Lake".

Changbai Mountains derived its name from white pumice stones and accumulated snow on its main Baitou Mountain (White-headed Mountain). Heavenly Lake is surrounded by 16 magnificent precipitous mountain peaks. The water flows into the lake from the north and rushes over 70-meter high steep cliffs, creating the famous Changbai Mountain Waterfall, which has the largest vertical drop of all the crater-lake waterfalls in the world. It is known as "the River to Heaven" because the waterfall resembles a leaning ladder to heaven in distance. The constant roaring sound of the plunging waterfall can be heard from miles away.

The weather in Changbai Mountains is cold and unpredictable. The changes in the lake can be erratic with quiet water, nice sunshine and gentle wind in the morning, and terrifying storms and waves in the afternoon.

> 堰塞湖

镜泊湖

镜泊湖位于黑龙江省宁安市西南，在唐朝时名“忽汗海”，明代始称“镜泊湖”，意为清平如镜，清代称其为“毕尔腾湖”，如今仍名“镜泊湖”。大约在一万年以前，火山活动使大量的玄武岩浆喷溢而出，熔岩流自西向东将牡丹江拦腰截断，于是形成镜泊湖。全湖分为北湖、中湖、南湖和上湖四个湖区。湖形狭长，为西南—东北走向，呈“S”形，蜿蜒曲折。湖水南浅北深，南北长45千米，东西最宽处6千米，面积约91.5平方千米，贮水量约11.8亿立方米。镜泊湖的湖面海拔为350米，是中国最大、世界第二大的高山堰塞湖。湖岸多港湾，湖中大小岛屿星罗棋布，景色优

> Barrier Lakes

Jingpo Lake

Jingpo Lake is located in the southwest of Ning'an City, Heilongjiang Province. Earlier names for Jingpo Lake include Huhanhai Lake in the Tang Dynasty and Bi'erteng Lake in the Qing Dynasty. The name Jingpo originated in the Ming Dynasty meaning as clear and smooth as a mirror and has been used till the present day. The lake formed about 10,000 years ago when large quantities of basaltic lava from volcanic eruptions in the region blocked the Mudanjiang River from east to west. Jingpo Lake is divided into north, south, central and upper lake areas. The long and narrow lake winds into an S-shape from southwest to northeast, shallower in the south and deeper in the north. It is 45 kilometers long from south to north and 6 kilometers wide from east to west covering a total of 91.5 square

● **镜泊湖**（图片提供：全景正片）

Jingpo Lake

美，被誉为“北方的西湖”。

镜泊湖尤以吊水楼瀑布最为著名，它位于镜泊湖的最北端。熔岩浆凝结成大坝阻塞了湖水北流，于是湖水便落入由熔岩坑塌陷而形成的深潭之中，形成大瀑布。瀑布落差约20米，宽40多米，水流湍急，酷似世界闻名的尼亚加拉大瀑布。由于其落差大，1000米以外就能听到轰隆隆的水声。吊水楼瀑布两侧悬崖巍峨陡峭，怪岩嶙峋峥嵘。冬季枯水期，熔岩床上会出现许多大小深浅不等的圆柱形溶洞，这是因为瀑布下的石块受到冲击，年深日久遂成光滑圆润的圆柱形溶洞，十分精巧别致。

镜泊湖附近还有许多文物古迹，如唐代渤海国上京故城遗址。渤海国是唐代中国东北部靺鞨粟末部联合其他靺鞨诸部所建立的地方政权，上京城即是其都城。上京城建制、规模完全仿照唐长安城建造，呈长方形。城中套城，分外城、内城和宫城三部分。外城为居民住宅区；内城在外城北部中央，为官衙和官僚住宅区；宫城在内城北部正中，宫殿在宫城中间。宫殿和房屋建筑材料多用石料和砖瓦，

kilometers with a water storage capacity of 1.18 billion cubic meters. At 350 meters in elevation, Jingpo Lake is the largest alpine barrier lake in China and the second largest alpine barrier lake in the world. The beautiful scenery of many bays and islands of different sizes has won Jingpo Lake the fame as "the West Lake of the North".

The most famous attraction of the lake is the Diaoshuilou Falls at the very northern end of the lake. When lava solidification built up and blocked the water flowing to the north, a big waterfall formed as the water plunged over a sheer precipice into the deep caldera. The waterfall is over 40 meters wide with a drop of 20 meters. The rapid water flow is similar to that of world-renowned Niagara Falls. The rumbling sound from the big water drop can be heard over 1,000 meters away. There are precipitous cliffs and grotesque rocks on either side of the waterfall. During the winter dry season, many cylindrical caves of various sizes and depths emerge on the lava bed. These smooth and unique lava tubes are the results of long lasting impact from the waterfall on the rocks below.

Around Jingpo Lake there are many cultural relics and heritage sites such as

吊水楼瀑布（图片提供：全景正片）
Diaoshuilou Falls

有宝相纹花砖、文字瓦、莲花瓦当，还有各种釉瓦等。从现在保留下来的遗址还可以想象当年上京城的繁华景象。

the ruins of the capital of the ancient Bohai Kingdom, a local regime established by the Mohe ethnic group in northeast China during the Tang Dynasty. The establishment and scale of the city was completely modeled after Chang'an, the capital of Tang. It was a rectangular-shaped city of cities dividing into outer city, inner city and palace city. Commoners resided in the outer city; officials lived in the inner city in the center of the northern section of the outer city; the palace compound was built in the center of the northern section of the inner city using mostly stones, decorative bricks and glazed tiles. One can imagine how prosperous this city might look in ancient times.

火山口原始森林及熔岩隧道

从镜泊湖北端西行50千米，即是世界著名的火山口原始森林。登上火山顶就会看到10个硕大的火山口，其中尤以3号火山口最大，直径达550米，深达200米。地下森林就生长在这些火山口圆形大坑中，水曲松、紫椴、水曲柳、黄花松、鱼鳞松等珍贵树种分布其中，还生长有人参、黄芪等中药材。树一般高20多米，最高达40米。森林总面积达669平方千米，是一座天然的绿色宝库。

在距地下森林约13千米的东南方，有几处海内外罕见的熔岩隧道。据推算，熔岩隧道是几万年前火山喷发时形成的。炽热奔腾的熔岩流沿河谷而下，熔岩表层在空气中冷却凝成硬壳，而内部仍处于高温流动状态，遂形成地下熔岩河。当火山停止喷发，岩浆源断流时，熔岩流内部出现巨大的地下空洞，便形成熔岩隧道。这里最长的隧道在500米以上，一般宽5米多，高3米。隧道顶呈拱形，表面为黑紫色，顶部布满下垂欲滴的熔岩乳，地面随处可见石柱、石床、石阶等，形态各异，鬼斧神工。

• 火山口原始森林（图片提供：全景正片）
Caldera Virgin Forest

Caldera Virgin Forest and Lava Tunnels

The world famous caldera virgin forest is located 50 kilometers to the northwest of Jingpo Lake. At the top of the volcano are ten enormous craters among which Crater 3 is the largest with a diameter of 550 meters and a depth of 200 meters. An underground forest is thriving in these craters full of rare plant species such as shuiqu pine, Manchurian ash, yellow pine and ichthyosis pine as well as Ginseng, astragalus and other Chinese herbs. The average height of a tree is over 20 meters with the tallest reaching 40 meters. Covering a total area of 669 square kilometers, this forest is indeed a natural green treasure house.

There are several lava tunnels rarely seen in the world about 13 kilometers to the southeast of the underground forest. Tens of thousands of years ago during volcano eruptions, lava tubes formed when the hot lava flowed on the surface became thickened in the cold air and turned into a hard crust above the still-flowing underground lava stream. When the supply of lava stopped at the end of the eruption, partially empty cave-like conduits beneath the ground became the lava tunnels. The longest tunnel is over 500 meters with an average width of over 5 meters and a height of 3 meters. The arched ceiling of the tunnel has a dark purple surface filled with dripping lavacicles. A variety of lava pillars, beds and steps can be seen everywhere on the floor of the tunnel which are of different shapes and forms.

五大连池

五大连池位于黑龙江省五大连池市境内，小兴安岭西南侧，是中国仅次于镜泊湖的第二大高山堰塞湖。18世纪初期，大规模的火山喷发致使大量岩浆外溢，熔岩流堵塞了白河河道并将其隔断，于是形成了5个串珠状的湖泊，“五大连池”也因此得名。五大连池由头池、二池、三池、四池和五池组成，五池相连，长5250米，总面积为26.2平

Wudalianchi

Wudalianchi (Five Connected Lakes) is the second largest alpine barrier lake next to Jingpo Lake in China, located to the southwest of Lesser Khingan Range in Wudalianchi City, Heilongjiang Province. In the beginning of the 18th century, basalt lava from volcano eruptions blocked the watercourse of Baihe River and broke the river up into a series of five connected lakes, hence the name "Five Connected Lakes". Wudalianchi consists of the head lake, second, third, fourth and

方千米。其中三池最大，面积达8.4平方千米；头池最小，面积仅0.18平方千米；二池最深，达12米；头池最浅，水深2米。五大连池池水清澈，有丰富的矿泉水资源，素有“神泉”之誉。这里的水多为冷矿泉，水中含有十几种对人体有益的元素。

五大连池火山群由14座火山锥、一系列的盾状火山和大面积的熔岩流组成。这里拥有世界上保存最完整、品类最齐全、状貌最典型的火山地质地貌。老黑山附近有

fifth lake with a length of 5,250 meters and a total area of 26.2 square kilometers. The third lake is the largest covering 8.4 square kilometers while the head lake is the smallest with an area of 0.18 square kilometers. The second lake is the deepest at 12 meters in depth and the head lake, the shallowest, is only 2 meters deep. Wudalianchi has clear water and a rich mineral water resource. Known as the "magic spring", Wudalianchi produces mostly cold mineral spring containing a dozen elements beneficial for human health.

五大连池风光（图片提供：全景正片）
Scenery of Wudalianchi

一块岩浆凝成的黑色岩石，长17千米，最宽处12千米，面积70多平方千米，被称做“石海”。石海景观奇特，熔岩造型变化万千，有的像大象，有的像老虎，有的像狗熊，还有的像瀑布，各种形象惟妙惟肖。这是由于岩浆在流动过程中，表层岩浆首先凝固形成光滑的岩溶表壳，而内部的岩浆流仍在运动，熔岩表层受岩浆流的牵引作用而形成的姿态万千的熔岩地貌。

九寨沟的“海子”

九寨沟位于四川省阿坝藏族羌族自治州九寨沟县漳扎镇，是川西北岷山山脉中一条纵深40多千米的山沟谷地，呈“丫”字形，从海拔1800米的沟口到海拔3000米左右的沟顶，串珠式地分布着108个大大小小形状各异的湖泊，当地人称为“海子”。

九寨沟的海子多属于堰塞湖，也有少数属于冰川湖。九寨沟一带位于地震带之上，由于地震引起的山崩碎石堵塞山谷，山地流水和地下水聚集堤内，从而形成湖泊。如今在长海和五花海附近，仍然可

The cluster of volcanoes in Wudalianchi consists of 14 volcanic cones, a series of shield volcanoes and large lava fields, which are considered the most well-preserved, the most complete and the most typical volcanic landform in the world. Near Laohei Mountain a black lava field called *Shihai* (Sea of Rocks) spreads out covering an area of over 70 square kilometers with a length of 17 kilometers and a maximum width of 12 kilometers. The unique landscape of *Shiha* shows varieties of volcanic rocks resembling elephants, tigers, bears and waterfalls. During the cooling and solidification process of flowing lava, different rock formations take shape when lava is still moving beneath the smooth solidified crust.

Lakes in Jiuzhaigou

Jiuzhaigou (Valley of Nine Villages) is situated in Zhangzha Town, Jiuzhaigou County of Ngawa Tibetan and Qiang Autonomous Prefecture, Sichuan Province. A more than 40-kilometer long valley in the Beimin Mountain Range west of Sichuan Province, the Y-shaped Jiuzhaigou stretches from its entrance at 1,800 meters in elevation to its top at an

• "童话世界"九寨沟（图片提供：全景正片）
Jiuzhaigou, the World of Fairy Tales

以看到地震后留下的众多堆积物。九寨沟流水中含有丰富的碳酸钙，当水流遇阻时，碳酸钙就会沉积下来，日积月累，便形成了乳白色的坚固钙质堤埂。流水蓄积堤内，从而形成众多的湖泊。树正群海就是这样形成的。

altitude of around 3,000 meters. There is a distribution of 108 lakes of different shapes and sizes in Jiuzhaigou and the local people call them "Haizi" meaning "sons of sea".

Most lakes in Jiuzhaigou are barrier lakes and a few are glacial lakes. As Jiuzhaigou is located above the seismic

古时九寨沟一带被称为“翠海”，它的海子各具特色。长海海拔3060米，长7千米，宽约1千米，形状为“S”形，是九寨沟最大、海拔最高的海子。周围山峰常年积雪，岸边树木枝繁叶茂，在山与树的衬托下，湖水更显清碧。长海岸边有一株巨大的“独臂老人柏”，由于长年风化，树左侧枝叶全无，右侧却枝叶挺茂。五花海位于日则沟孔雀河上游的尽头，海拔2472米，是九寨沟色彩最为绚烂的一个海子。海底由于钙化沉积，同一片

- 五花海

Wuhuahai (Five-flower Lake)

zone, these lakes formed as water from mountains and underground rivers began to accumulate in the valley dammed by rocks and gravels from earthquakes. A lot of debris left after the earthquake is still visible in *Changhai* (Long Sea) and *Wuhuahai* (Five-flower Lake). The water in Jiuzhaigou has high concentration of calcium carbonate. When the water flow was stopped in the dammed valley, calcium carbonate deposits in the water gradually became white dolomite embankments. Many ribbon lakes such as *Shuzheng Qunhai* Valley formed as water accumulated in these naturally dammed areas.

In ancient times, the Jiuzhaigou area was known as "the Emerald Sea" with each lake having its own characteristics. The S-shaped *Changhai* (Long Lake) is 7 kilometers long and 1 kilometer wide at an altitude of 3,060 meters. It is the highest and largest lake in Jiuzhaigou. The lake displays a clear and green color with the backdrop of snowcapped mountains and lush forests. A huge pine tree stands on the lakeside resembling a one-armed old man for it has profuse foliage on the right side and nothing on the weathered left side. *Wuhuahai* is at the upstream of Peacock River in

诺日朗瀑布
Nuorilang Falls

水域呈现出翠黄、墨绿、宝蓝、藏青等不同的颜色。天鹅海为半沼泽湖泊，海面上长满湖草和野花，水草肥美，每年都会有大量天鹅来这里栖息繁殖，天鹅海也因此得名。熊猫海面积约9万平方米，经常有熊猫来这里觅食、喝水。岸边有一块浑圆的大白石，上面还分布有天然的黑色斑纹，犹如憨态可掬的大熊猫，甚是可爱。

由于地势差异，湖与湖之间形

Rize Valley, 2,472 meters above the sea level. Known as the lake with the most splendid colors, *Wuhuahai* displays a multi-colored water surface of yellow green, dark green, sapphire blue and dark blue due to calcium deposits at the lake bottom. *Tian'ehai* (Swan Lake) is a semi-marsh lake covered with lake grasses and wildflowers. It is a breeding habitat for large numbers of swans every year thanks to its abundant water resources, hence the name Swan Lake. *Xiongmaohai* (Panda

珍珠滩瀑布（图片提供：全景正片）
Zhenzhutan Falls (Pearl Shoal Falls)

成许多瀑布，这些瀑布各具韵味。千姿百态的飞瀑、流泉与众多的海子动静结合，将108个湖泊连缀为一体，刚柔相济，达到出神入化的境界。诺日朗瀑布海拔2365米，高

Lake) covers an area of 900 square kilometers where pandas were said to have come here to drink and eat. A big white round rock sitting on the lakeside has natural black stripes resembling a lovely giant panda.

24.5米，宽270米，水流湍急，水声震耳，是中国最宽的瀑布。珍珠滩瀑布高21米，宽162米，海拔2443米，瀑布水势凶猛，溅起的水如天女散花般撒落下来，在阳光照射下如晶莹剔透的珍珠。熊猫海瀑布高78米，宽50米，为九寨沟落差最大的瀑布，变化多样，时而细腻，时而洒脱。

扎如寺位于九寨沟之中的扎如沟宝镜崖下，距今已有1000多年的历史，建筑结构精巧，具有明显的藏族风格，屋脊金顶闪光，佛像庄严神圣。整个建筑群包括大殿、藏经楼、乐台、房、库房、迎客楼、喇嘛居室七个部分。

羊卓雍错

羊卓雍错，位于西藏自治区浪卡子县境内，藏语意为“碧玉”“草原之湖”，简称“羊湖”。很多年以前，喜马拉雅运动使青藏高原不断隆起，出现了一条巨大的断裂带。后来冰川泥石流堵塞了河道，从而形成了形状很不规则的羊卓雍错。羊卓雍错的湖岸蜿蜒曲折，分叉较多，湖岸线长达250

The difference in Jiuzhaigou terrains created many spectacular waterfalls connecting 108 lakes into one magical scene of harmony between rapid water flows and tranquil lakes. Nuorilang Falls at 2,365 meters in elevation are the widest waterfall in China with a height of 24.5 meters and a width of 270 meters. The rapid water flow at Nuorilang Falls produces a deafening sound. Zhenzhutan Falls (Pearl Shoal Falls) is 21 meters tall and 162 meters wide at 2,443 meters in elevation. The raging water plunges into the shoal splashing shining water drops everywhere as if they were pearls under the sun or flowers scattering by fairies. The multi-stream and multi-level Panda Lake Falls are 78 meters high and 50 meters wide having the largest drop in Jiuzhaigou.

The Zharu Temple is located under the Baojing Cliff (Precious Mirror Cliff) of Zharu Valley in Jiuzhaigou. With a history of over 1,000 years, the temple's exquisite building structure embodies a strong Tibetan style. The entire compound consists of seven quarters including the big hall, a sutra library, a music room, a guest house, a storage room, monks' residence and some miscellaneous rooms.

千米，面积638平方千米，是西藏三大圣湖之一，也是西藏南部最大的内陆湖泊。

羊卓雍错的周围还分布着空姆错、沉错和纠错三小湖，它们如同四个姐妹手足相连，难分难舍。从高空俯瞰会发现这些湖泊犹如耳坠，镶嵌在山的耳郭之上，因此羊卓雍错又有“神女散落的绿松石耳坠”之称。

• 羊卓雍错
Yamdrok Lake

Yamdrok Lake

Yamdrok Lake means "green jade" or "lake on the grassland" in Xizang with an abbreviated name of Yam Lake. It is located at Nagarzê County, Tibet Autonomous Region. Many years ago, a huge fault zone appeared as a result of continuous rising of Qinghai-Tibet Plateau caused by the Himalayan movement. The irregular-shaped Yamdrok Lake formed in the fault zone riverbed dammed by glacier mudslides. The mountainous lakeshore is highly crenellated with a 250-kilometer circumference covering an area of 638 square kilometers. It is one of the three holy lakes in Xizang and the largest inland lake in south Xizang.

Around the Yamdrok Lake are three smaller lakes. They are so close together as if they were four sisters hard to separate from one another. In an aerial view the lakes look like earrings on the mountain earlobes. That is why Yamdrok Lake is also known as the "turquoise earrings lost by fairies".

Yamdrok is considered a holy place and highly respected by Tibetans. According to legends, one year during the Tibetan Bathing Festival, a Tara

羊卓雍错在藏族同胞的心目中有着无比崇高、神圣的地位。传说有一年在藏族的传统节日沐浴节时，度母曾来湖中洗澡，此后她便成为"圣母"。羊卓雍错也因此被称为"圣湖"。

宁金抗沙峰凌驾于圣湖之上，是拉轨岗日山的主峰，海拔7206米，是西藏中部四大雪山之一。山上坡岭沟壑间有众多冰川，时常有雪崩发生。著名的卡若拉冰川就在它的南麓。

Buddha bathed in this lake and became the female Guardian of Buddhism. Since then Yamdrok Lake began to be known as a holy lake.

Over the sacred lake stands the Ningjin Kangsha Peak with an elevation of 7,206 meters. It is the main peak of Lhagoi Kangri Mountain, one of the four big snowcapped mountains in central Xizang. Glaciers developed in many of the mountain's valleys and gullies where avalanches happen frequently. The famous Karola Glacier is located at the mountain's southern foothills.

• **拉轨岗日山**（图片提供：全景正片）
Lhagoi Kangri Mountain

> 冰川湖

喀纳斯湖

喀纳斯湖位于新疆维吾尔自治区阿勒泰地区布尔津县北部，是一个坐落在深山密林中的高山湖泊。它是由巨大的冰川刨蚀而成，至今，在湖东岸还可以看到留有冰川擦痕的羊背石。“喀纳斯”在蒙古语里是“美丽富饶而神秘”的意思，湖面海拔1374米，湖长25千米，宽1.6千米，总面积45.73平方千米。喀纳斯湖呈月牙状，湖东岸为弯月的内侧，沿岸有6道向湖心凸出的岩石平台，形成6道湾。湖面会随着季节和天气的变化而变换颜色，因此有“变色湖”之称。

在湖的最北端，有一条千米枯木长堤。当湖水上涨时，枯木长堤

> Glacial Lakes

Kanas Lake

Kanas Lake is located to the north of Burqin County in Altay Prefecture, Xinjiang Uyghur Autonomous Region. Laying in the deep mountain range of dense forests, it is an alpine lake formed by enormous glacier corrosion. Roche moutonnee or sheepback rocks created by the passing of the glacier can still be seen in the eastern lakeshore. Kanas means "rich, beautiful, and mysterious" in Mongolian. The lake covers a total of 45.73 square kilometers with a length of 25 kilometers, a width of 1.6 kilometers and an elevation of 1,374 meters. The crescent moon shaped lake has 6 rock platforms extending to the center of the lake along the east shoreline. The lake displays different colors following seasonal and weather

● **喀纳斯湖**（图片提供：全景正片）
Kanas Lake

会逆流而上，长长地横在喀纳斯湖的6道湾上。据说有人曾将枯木扔到下游，但是枯木依然会自己逆流飘到上游。经研究发现，强劲的山谷风在遇到喀纳斯湖南面的巨大山体后，风力转向，推动枯木逆流上漂，日积月累逐渐在湖口会聚堆叠就形成了一条百余米宽、两千米长的枯木长堤。

changes, hence the name "the color changing lake".

To the very northern end of the lake lies a couple of thousand meters long embankment of dead tree logs. When the water in the lake rises, the dead trees float up against the stream and pile up along the six peninsulas in the upper reaches. It is said that people intentionally threw some dead trees in

在每年的8月份左右，当太阳升到一定高度时，在湖西山谷的云雾中会逐渐显现出一个半圆形的巨大彩色光环。随着太阳高度和云雾浓淡的变化，光环色泽时深时浅，时明时暗，大约可以持续一刻钟左右。

在喀纳斯湖景区，还能看到各种各样的岩画。如山羊、野猪、刺猬、雪鸡、马、羊、鹿、狼等动物造型岩画，还有狩猎、征战、放

the lower reaches, but they still floated against the current to the upper reaches. According to some studies, these dead trees are pushed against the current to upper reaches by extremely strong valley wind from south of the Kanas Lake when the wind hits the huge mountain and changes its course. With the elapse of time piles of dead trees formed this 2000-meter-long and over 100-meter-wide embankment.

Each year around August when

• **图瓦人的村落**（图片提供：全景正片）
A Tuvan Village

牧、舞蹈以及图腾崇拜岩画等。其中最大的一幅岩画为梅花鹿图案，造型优美，手法细腻。这些岩画反映了中国古代游牧民族的真实生活，对研究古代社会史、民族史具有重要的价值。

喀纳斯湖畔生活着图瓦人——属蒙古人种。至今图瓦人一直保持着比较原始的生活方式。他们的房子是用松木搭盖成的尖斜顶的小木屋，木屋由粗大的原木相叠而成。图瓦人能歌善舞，马头琴是他们最喜爱的乐器。每年的6月，图瓦

• 在敖包节上表演歌舞的图瓦姑娘

（图片提供：FOTOE）

Tuvan Women Dancing in Aobao Festival

the sun rises to a certain height, a huge semicircular colorful halo will gradually appear in the clouds in the valley to the west of the lake. The halo turns darker or lighter for about 15 minutes depending on the changes in the height of the sun and the density of the clouds.

In the lake's scenic areas, there are a variety of rock paintings of goats, wild boars, hedgehogs, snow chickens, horses, sheep, deer and wolves as well as paintings of hunting, fighting, herding, dancing and totem worships. The largest rock painting depicts spotted deer in an elegant and delicate way. These rock paintings not only reflect the life of ancient Chinese nomads, but also have important value in the study of ancient societies and ethnic histories.

Kanas Lake is mostly inhabited by Tuvans from the Mongolian designation. Even today they still maintain a primitive lifestyle. A Tuvan house is built in large pine logs and has a pointed pitched roof. Tuvans are good at dancing and singing and their most favorable music instrument is *Matouqin*, a fiddle with the top carved like a horse's head. Every year in June, the Tuvans have the Aobao Festival with lots of entertainment and

人都要举行一次大型的娱乐体育活动——敖包节，进行骑马、射箭、摔跤等比赛，开展祭山、祭天、祭火、祭树、祭鱼等活动，并且还要拜佛诵经。

sports activities of riding, wrestling and archery. Religious activities are also conducted including chanting of Buddhist sutra and rituals to pay respect to mountains, heaven, fire, trees and fish.

罗布泊

罗布泊，古称“蒲昌海”“盐泽”等，因地处古代丝绸之路要冲而著称于世。它位于新疆维吾尔自治区塔里木盆地的最低处，面积曾达5350平方千米，曾是中国第二大内陆湖。今天的罗布泊已经彻底干涸，没有任何生命迹象，被称为“死亡之海”。干涸的罗布泊呈现的耳朵形状，耳轮、耳孔、耳垂清晰可见，这使得罗布泊更加神秘。

• 罗布泊
Lop Nur

提起罗布泊，人们总会想到楼兰古城。据记载，历史上的楼兰物产丰富，经济富庶，是丝绸之路上的繁华之邦。如今的楼兰只剩下了断壁残垣。1980年，著名的“楼兰美女”被发现，这是一具保存完好的女性古尸，皮肤为古铜色，还稍有弹性，头发细密，面部瘦削，眼睛大而深，鼻梁尖高，下巴尖而翘。由于这具尸体是在神秘的楼兰古城附近被发现的，所以就给她取名为“楼兰美女”。这种种的发现，让楼兰古城更具神秘色彩。

Lop Nur

Lop Nur (Lop Lake) used to be the second largest endorheic lake in China, located at the lowest part of Tarim Basin in Xinjiang Uygur Autonomous Region covering an area of 5350 square kilometers. The Lop Nur area was once a well-known trading hub in the ancient Silk Road. The lake's ancient names include "Puchang Sea" and "Salt Lake". Today's Lop Nur is totally desiccated without any signs of life; therefore it is also called "Sea of Death". The present Lop Nur dried basin has a shape of an ear with visibly defined ear holes and earlobes, which make the lake even more mysterious.

The ancient city of Loulan or Kroran is found around the Lop Nur region. According to historical documents, Loulan was once a kingdom of rich natural resources and economic prosperity on the Silk Road. Today only ruins of the town remain. In 1980 the famous "Beauty of Loulan" mummy was discovered. The female mummy was preserved in very good condition with a brownish skin color, delicate and dense hair, an angular face, recessed eyes and a big nose. The mummy was found near the ancient city of Loulan, hence the name "Beauty of Loulan". These archeological discoveries have added more mysteries to this ancient city.

> 河成湖

白洋淀

白洋淀位于河北省保定市，是中国海河平原上最大的湖泊，面积336平方千米，素有“华北明珠”之称。大约7000万年以前，白洋淀所在之处还是一片汪洋大海，后来太行山区冲刷下来的泥沙不断淤积，海水变浅，低洼处由于海河水的漫延和长期淤积，排水不畅，长年累月，滞水成湖。这里现有大小淀泊百余个，其中以白洋淀、羊角淀、池鱼淀较大，总称“白洋淀”。淀中的园田、村庄像小岛一样星罗棋布，纵横相连。

白洋淀风景绝美，以水、芦苇、荷花、香蒲为主的水乡景观独具特色。每年的7月—9月，白洋

> Fluvial Lakes

Baiyangdian

Baiyangdian (Baiyang Lake) located in Baoding City, Hebei Province is the largest lake in China's Haihe River Plain covering a total of 336 square kilometers known as the "Pearl of North China". About 70 million years ago, this region was a vast ocean. Later due to constant mudslides from Taihang Mountain range, the ocean gradually became shallow, the silt piled up on the flooded plain and lakes formed as water accumulated in the low-lying land. There are more than 100 lakes of different sizes in this region among which the larger ones are Baiyang, Yangjiao and Chiyu lakes. This group of lakes is called Baiyangdian collectively. The entire lake region is dotted with villages and reed marshes crisscrossed by thousands of rivers and ditches.

淀的荷花层层叠叠，亭亭玉立，分外好看。秋天的白洋淀独具魅力，大量的芦苇杂生在荷花地里，闪着银光的芦穗儿在风中摇摆，阵风吹来，犹如成群的白羊在奔跑。

白洋淀水产资源丰富，是有名的淡水鱼场，盛产鲑鱼、鲤鱼、青鱼、虾、河蟹等，其中以圆鱼、桂花鱼最为有名。芦苇是白洋淀的著名物产，产量大，皮薄色佳，韧性好，用它编织成的席、箔，柔软光滑，坚固耐用，因此素有“鱼苇

The enchanting scenery of Baiyangdian is mainly featured by the water, reeds, lotus flowers and cattail. Every year from July to September, Baiyangdian displays layers upon layers of gorgeous lotus flowers. In the fall, visitors are greeted with a unique charming sight of densely grown reeds in the oases of lotuses and silver reed panicles swinging in the wind as if white sheep were running on the pasture.

Rich in aquatic resources, Baiyangdian is a well-known freshwater fish farm which produces salmons, red carps, black

• **白洋淀**（图片提供：全景正片）
Baiyangdian

• **白洋淀的荷花**（图片提供：全景正片）
Lotus Flowers in Baiyangdian

之乡”之称。另外淀里水生植物遍布，野鸭、大雁栖息。人们可以捕捞鱼虾，采挖莲藕。一年四季，一片繁忙。所以人们也称其为“日进斗金、四季皆秋”的聚宝盆。

洪泽湖

洪泽湖位于淮河下游、江苏省洪泽县西部，发育在淮河中游的冲

carps and river crabs. The most famous are soft-shelled turtles and Chinese perch. Another renowned product of Baiyangdian is the abundantly yielded high-quality reeds. Their softness, smoothness and durability make reeds a good material for weaving mats and curtains. Therefore, it also known as "lake of fish and reeds". The lake is also a habitat for wild ducks and wild geese. People can go fishing or harvesting lotus

积平原上，为中国第四大淡水湖。它原是泄水不畅的洼地，后积水形成许多小湖，唐代始名“洪泽湖”。北宋（960—1127）时，洪泽运河开通，使淮河与湖区相连。明清时期由于黄河泥沙淤积在淮河，河水排水不畅，致使洪泽湖积水日甚，湖面扩大。现在湖长65千米，平均宽约24.4千米，水深一般在4米以内，面积为2069平方千米，

roots all year round here, so they describe Baiyangdian as a lake of treasures where "every season is a harvest season and money can be made every day".

Hongze Lake

Hongze Lake is the fourth largest freshwater lake in China located at the lower reaches of Huaihe River west of Hongze County, Jiangsu Province. It was originally a basin with hardly any water

• **洪泽湖**（图片提供：FOTOE）
Hongze Lake

• **镇水铁牛**（图片提供：FOTOE）
洪泽湖镇水铁牛，安放在大堤险要地段。铁牛身长1.70米、宽0.57米、高0.68米，厚0.07米的一块铁板与牛身铸为一体，共重约2250公斤（也有人说重4000公斤）。

Iron Ox to Suppress Flooding

The iron ox is placed in a crucial location of the levee as a symbol to suppress flooding. The iron ox is 1.7 meters long, 0.57 meters wide and 0.68 meters tall. It is cast together with a 0.07-meter thick iron plate reaching a total weight of 2,250 kilograms (some said that it weighs 4,000 kilograms).

由三大湖湾组成。洪泽湖为一“悬湖”，即湖底高出东部下河平原4—8米。湖区东部的大堤蜿蜒曲折共108弯，全部由玄武岩条石砌成，宽50米，长67千米，是下游地区的重要安全保障。

明祖陵坐落于洪泽湖西畔，是明朝开国皇帝朱元璋的高祖、曾祖、祖父三代人的陵墓，被称为

outlets on the alluvial plain in the middle reaches of Huaihe River. Therefore water accumulation in the basin resulted in many small lakes. The name Hongze began in the Tang Dynasty. In the Northern Song Dynasty (960-1127) Hongze Canal was built to connect the lakes to Huaihe River. In the Ming and Qing dynasties, sediment deposition from the Yellow River gradually silted up Huaihe River and with no direct outlet to the sea the water accumulation in the river expanded the lake's surface area. The present lake consists of three bays and covers an area of 2,069 square kilometers with a length of 65 kilometers, an average width of 24.4 kilometers and an average depth of less than 4 meters. Hongze Lake is considered a "hanging lake" as the lake bottom is 4-8 meters above the plain in the eastern lower reaches. The huge levee in the east of the lake is all built with Basalt stone slabs. It is 67 kilometers long and 50 kilometers wide winding through 108 turns. The levee is an important safeguard for the lower reach regions.

The Ming Ancestral Tombs are located at the western shore of Hongze Lake. Known as the "first tombs of the Ming Dynasty", they are tombs of the grandfather, great grandfather, and great-great grandfather of Emperor Zhu

明祖陵石雕（图片提供：全景正片）

Stone Statues of the Ming Ancestral Tombs

"明代第一陵"。祖陵神道长达250米，神道两侧有望柱二对，石像十九对，气势不凡。文臣、武将、狮子、麒麟、马等造型生动优美，栩栩如生，精雕细刻，精美绝伦。洪泽湖南岸，淮河入湖处有一座山，名"老子山"。相传老子曾在此炼丹，所以又称"丹山"。在山上，依然可以看到炼丹台、青牛蹄和凤凰墩等遗迹。

Yuanzhang, the founding emperor of the Ming Dynasty. The tombs' Spirit Way (*Shendao*, the path to the tomb entrance) is 250 meters long sided by two pairs of stone pillars and nineteen pairs of carved stone animals and human figures. These stone statues of lions, horses, unicorns, imperial civil officials and generals are life-like and exquisite. According to legends Laozi lived on Mount Laozi at southern lakeshore to make elixir of immortality so it also known as Mount Elixir. Today the ruins of the platform where he practiced alchemy and other related sites still exist.

> 海成湖

西湖

西湖位于浙江省杭州市的西面，一直以来，就以秀丽的山水与众多的人文景观著称于世，被誉为“天下第一湖”，也被誉为“人间天堂”。汉代传说金牛曾在湖中涌现，故称为“金牛湖”。隋唐时称“钱塘湖”，又因湖在城西，故称“西湖”。北宋时，因大文学家苏轼把西湖比作美女西施，又称“西子湖”。

据地质学家和古地理学家的研究，在距今约1万年前，西湖还只是一个和杭州湾相通的浅海湾。春秋战国时期，今杭州市区仍是随海潮出没的沙滩。在漫长的岁月中，由海潮和钱塘江、长江携带来的泥沙在海湾口两侧滞留沉积下来，将海

> Shoreline Lakes

West Lake

West Lake *Xi Hu* is located in the west side of Hangzhou City, Zhejiang Province. Famous for its picturesque landscape and cultural heritage, the lake has always been known as "the Paradise on Earth" and the "No. 1 Lake under Heaven". It was once called "Lake of Golden Ox" based on a Han Dynasty legend that a golden ox once merged from the lake. In the Sui and Tang dynasties, the lake was first known as "Qiantang Lake" and later "West Lake" based on the location of the lake in Hangzhou. In the Northern Song Dynasty, the literary master Su Shi named it "Xizi Lake" when he compared the lake to the famous ancient beauty Xishi (a.k.a. Xizi) in his poem.

According to geological and paleogeographical studies, West Lake

西湖白堤春色
White Dyke Spring Scenery of West Lake in Hangzhou

湾隔断，形成一个潟湖，这就是西湖的前身。

西湖三面环山，略呈椭圆形，南北长约3.3千米，东西宽约2.8千米，面积约5.66平方千米。孤山是西湖中唯一的天然岛屿；夕照山的雷峰塔与宝石山的保俶塔隔湖相望；小瀛洲、湖心亭、阮公墩三个人工小岛卧于外西湖湖心；孤山、白堤、苏堤、杨公堤将湖面分隔为外

was originally a shallow gulf connecting to Hangzhou Bay. During the Spring and Autumn and Warring States periods, Hangzhou's downtown used to be a shoal moved by waves and tides. After many years sediments carried by the Yangtze River silted the gulf on both sides and formed a lagoon which became the predecessor of West Lake.

The slightly oval-shaped West Lake is surrounded by mountains in three sides.

西湖、西里湖（又称“后西湖”或“后湖”）、北里湖（又称“里西湖”）、小南湖（又称“南湖”）及岳湖等五片水面。于是形成了“一山、二塔、三岛、三堤、五湖”的基本格局。

It covers 5.66 square kilometers, 3.3 kilometers long from south to north and 2.8 kilometers from east to west. Gushan Island (Solitary Island) is the only natural island on the lake. Leifeng Pagoda on Sunset Hill directly faces Baochu Pagoda across the lake on Gem Hill. In

曲院风荷

夏日的西湖，最引人瞩目的要数曲院风荷公园里的大片荷花了，公园内大大小小的池子里栽满了上百个品种的荷花。南宋时期，西湖西侧有一座酿酒作坊，造出来的曲酒，享誉国内。每当夏日风起，酒香夹杂着荷香，扑面而来，沁人心脾，于是得名“曲院风荷”。

Breeze-ruffled Lotus at Quyuan Garden

West Lake's most attractive scenery in the summer is blooming lotus flowers. Over a hundred lotus species are planted in ponds of different sizes. In the Southern Song Dynasty, there was a brewery to the west of the lake making wine renowned in the country. The wine aroma and the lotus fragrance blended together in the summer breeze making people relaxed and refreshed, hence the name "Scent of the Brewery and Lotus in Summer Breeze".

孤山位于里湖与外湖之间，海拔约38米，面积约0.22平方千米，是湖中唯一的天然岛屿。小瀛洲位于西湖中部，是一个湖心岛，由疏浚西湖的淤泥堆积而成，面积约6万平方米，岛上建有亭、台、楼、榭，著名的“三潭印月”景观就在这里。湖心亭位于西湖中央，与安徽滁州的醉翁亭、北京先农坛的陶然

the center of the outer West Lake are three manmade islands: Xiaoyingzhou, Huxinting and Ruangongdun islands. GuShan Island, Bai and Su Causeways divide the lake surface into five areas: Outer West Lake, West Inner Lake, North Inner Lake, Little South Lake and Yuehu Lake. This layout is described as "one hill, two pagodas, three islands, three causeways and five lakes".

Gushan Island is situated between the inner and outer lakes covering 0.22 square kilometers with an elevation of 38 meters. The 60,000 square meters Xiaoyingzhou Island in the center of the

• 苏堤

宋朝大诗人苏轼在出任杭州地方官时，疏浚西湖，关心民生，颇有建树。他修建的堤坝由淤泥和葑草堆筑而成，取名为“苏堤”。苏堤两旁植有垂柳、碧桃、海棠、芙蓉、紫藤等四十多种花木。春日来临，新柳吐翠，微风拂面，美景如画，故称“苏堤春晓”。

Su Causeway

When he was the governor of Hangzhou, the Song Dynasty poet Su Shi made remarkable achievements in dredging West Lake for the people. Named after Su Shi, the Su Causeway was built with sediments and turnip grass from the lake. Over 40 plant species are planted along the causeway including willows, flowering peach, begonia, hibiscus and wisteria. The causeway displays picturesque scenery of blooming willow trees swaying in the spring breeze as the sun is about to rise, hence the name "Spring Dawn at Su Causeway".

lake was formed after a silt-dredging operation. Built with pagodas and pavilions this island is best-known for its scenic spot of "Three Ponds Mirroring the Moon". Located right in the center of the lake, Huxin (Lake Center) Pavilion is one of the four most famous pavilions in China. The other three are Zuiweng (Drunkard) Pavilion of Chuzhou, Anhui Province, Taoran Pavilion of Beijing and Aiwan Pavilion of Changsha, Hunan Province.

West Lake has ten most famous scenic spots, which became known in the Southern Song Dynasty. They are: Spring Dawn at Su Causeway, Lingering Snow on the Broken Bridge, Twin

• **三潭印月**

西南面湖中竖着三个造型美观的瓶形小石塔，三塔均高2米左右。每当皓月悬空，“月光印潭，影分为三”，塔里点上灯烛，烛光倒影湖中，像是月亮溶于水里，故名“三潭印月”。

Three Pools Mirroring the Moon

Located off the southern shore of the lake are three little charming vase-shaped stone pagodas with an average height of 2 meters. On evenings when the full moon shines on the lake, the moon light and the light of the candles placed inside the pagodas are all reflected on the waters as if four moons were shimmering together, hence the name "Three Pools Mirroring the Moon".

• 断桥

每当瑞雪初霁，西湖银装素裹。断桥两端白雪皑皑，远远望去，石桥身似隐似现，似断非断，故名“断桥残雪”。

Broken Bridge

Each year after the first snow, West Lake is all dressed up in white and the two ends of the bridge are covered with snow. When viewed from afar, the bridge seems to be half visible and half hidden sometimes as if it was broken in some sections, hence the name "Lingering Snow on the Broken Bridge".

亭、湖南长沙的爱晚亭并称中国四大名亭。

西湖有十景，这十景形成于南宋时期，分别为：苏堤春晓、断桥残雪、双峰插云、三潭印月、花港观鱼、柳浪闻莺、曲院风荷、平湖秋月、南屏晚钟、雷峰夕照。被这些景色点缀的西湖犹如一条斑斓的彩带，无论春夏秋冬还是阴晴雨雪都独有风韵。

Peaks Piercing the Clouds, Three Pools Mirroring the Moon, Viewing Fish at Flower Pond, Orioles Singing in the Willows, Breeze-ruffled Lotus at Quyuan Garden, Autumn Moon over the Calm Lake, Evening Bell Ringing at Nanping Hill, Leifeng Pagoda in the Evening Glow.With these views embellishment, West Lake is like a colorful ribbon. Regardless of seasons or vicissitudes, the lake has unique charm.

南湖

南湖位于浙江省嘉兴市南面，面积0.35平方千米，素以“轻烟拂渚，微风欲来”的迷人景色著称于世。很久以前，南湖还是一个被海水淹没的地方。长江和钱塘江携带的大量泥沙在入海口不断沉积，使陆地延伸，海水退出，后来运河各渠流水不断注入洼地而形成南湖。

South Lake

South Lake *Nan Hu* is situated in the south of Jiaxing City, Zhejiang Province covering an area of 0.35 square kilometers. The lake is well-known for its enchanting scenery of "misty rain amidst soft breeze". Long time ago, South Lake was still submerged under the sea water. As large amounts of sediments carried by the Yangtze River and Qiantang River

• **嘉兴南湖湖心岛**（图片提供：FOTOE）
Lake Center Islet on the South Lake, Jiaxing

烟雨楼（图片提供：全景正片）
Misty Rain Tower

南湖由运河各渠汇流而成，地形如同八卦，故又有“秀水福地”的雅称。

湖中有两个岛屿，一为湖心岛，一为小南湖。湖心岛位于南湖中心，南北长100多米，东西宽近100米，以烟雨楼为主体的古园林建筑群便坐落于此。烟雨楼自五代至今已有1000多年的历史。烟雨楼重檐画栋，朱柱明窗，登楼远眺，景色可尽收眼底。楼内保存着大量文人学士留下的字碑、石刻，具有相当高的文物价值。如宋朝四大书法家之一米芾的真迹诗碑、宋朝诗人

continuously deposited at its outlet to the sea, the sea water gradually subsided and the land area expanded. Later South Lake formed when the low-lying land was continuously fed by water from different river tributaries. It is known as an auspicious place because of its Eight Diagrams shape.

South Lake has two islets: the Lake Center Islet and the Little South Islet. The Lake Center Islet in the center of South Lake is over 100 meters long from south to north and 100 meters wide from east to west. There is a compound of ancient garden structures with the main building Misty Rain Tower on this islet. Built in

苏轼的“马券石刻”、元朝四大书画家之一吴镇的《风竹图》、清朝书法家冀应龙“烟雨楼”手迹等。小南湖位于南湖东北部，是湖中小岛，清代时由淤泥堆积而成。岛上还建有三间庙祠，供奉仓颉（传说中的中国汉字的造字鼻祖）。

湖心岛东南岸，停泊着一只长16米，宽3米的游船，这是根据中国共产党“一大”召开时用过的游艇仿制的纪念船。1921年，中国共产党第一次全国代表大会在这里顺利闭幕，庄严宣告了中国共产党的成立。

the Five dynasties, the thousand-year-old Misty Rain Tower has red pillars with painted carvings, double eaves and bright windows. At the top of the building one can enjoy a panoramic view of the lake. Steles and stone inscriptions left behind by many scholars are preserved in the tower. These cultural relics of very high values include the stele by Mi Fu, one of the four master calligraphers of the Song Dynasty, the stone inscription by the Song Dynasty poet Su Shi, the painting *Bamboo in the Wind* by Wu Zhen, one of the four master painters of the Yuan Dynasty and handwriting of "Misty Rain Tower" by the Qing Dynasty calligrapher Ji Yinglong. The Little South Lake, is a small islet in the northeast side of the lake formed by piled sediments in the Qing Dynasty. On the islet there are three temples of shrines for Cangjie, the inventor of the Chinese characters in legend.

A 16-meter-long and 3-meter-wide tour boat is anchored on the southeast shore of the Lake Center Islet. It is a commemorative copy of the boat used for the first national congress of the Communist Party of China, which in 1921 declared the birth of the Chinese Communist Party at the conference's conclusion.

> 人工湖

松花湖

松花湖位于吉林省吉林市东南郊，又名“丰满水库”，是因拦截松花江水修建丰满水电站而形成的大型湖泊，是东北地区最大的人工湖泊。湖面海拔266.5米，全长约200千米，最深达77.5米，总面积425平方千米，蓄水量可达108亿立方米。

湖面沿山谷呈狭长多弯之状，从空中俯瞰，松花湖就像一串闪光的珍珠，湖中有大小岛屿100多座。五虎岛是松花湖中最著名的一座岛屿，远看犹如五只东北虎嬉戏于湖水上。金龟岛，因其形状似一只凫于水上、有头有尾的大乌龟而得名。蘑菇岛在石龙壁下游，不但岛

> Artificial Lakes

Songhua Lake

Songhua Lake is located in the southeast suburbs of Jilin City, Jilin Province. Also known as Fengman Reservoir, it is the largest manmade lake in Northeast China, built when Songhua River was intercepted for the construction of Fengman Hydropower Station. The lake covers 425 square kilometers with a total length of 200 kilometers, the innermost depth of 77.5 meters, an elevation of 266.5 meters and a water storage capacity of up to 10.8 billion cubic meters.

The lake surface is long and narrow with many turns along the surrounding hills. There are over 100 islands of different sizes in the lake, and the lake looks like a string of shining pearls in an aerial view. The most famous attraction is the Five-tiger Island (*Wuhu Dao*) in

• **吉林松花湖**（图片提供：全景正片）
Songhua Lake, Jilin Province

形似蘑菇，而且岛上林木深处长满蘑菇。花砬子岛在湖的南部，岛上怪石林立，松柏挺秀。

阿什哈达摩崖碑位于松花湖下游的花岗岩峭壁上，是著名的古代摩崖石刻。碑分两处，均刻于明代。一处坐北朝南，刻于断崖

a shape resembling five tigers playing on the lake. The turtle-shaped Golden Turtle Island (*Jingui Dao*) floats on the water with a visible head and tail. The Mushroom Island (*Mogu Dao*) at the lower reaches is not only shaped like a mushroom, but also covered with mushrooms in the deep forests on the

绝壁之上，高1.35米；另一处坐东朝西，高1.22米。两碑相距约30米，两处摩崖碑均被筑亭保护。两碑经历了几百年的风雨，上面的字迹仍依稀可辨。碑上刻有明朝（1368—1644）朝廷官员在此处造船运兵运粮、修建龙王庙以及兵民罢工等史实，对研究当地历史具有重要作用。

island. To the south of the lake is Hualazi Island of grotesque rocks and magnificent pine trees.

The famous Ashidaimo ancient inscriptions are carved on the granite cliffs in the lower reaches of Songhua Lake. Both works of the Ming Dynasty, one inscription is 1.35 meters tall on a precipice facing south and the other one is 1.22 meters tall on a cliff facing west. The two 30-meter-apart cliff inscriptions

五虎岛（图片提供：FOTOE）
Five-tiger Island

昆明湖

颐和园主要由万寿山和昆明湖组成，是中国现存最大、保存最完整的皇家园林，位于北京市海淀区。昆明湖在颐和园万寿山南麓，属于半天然、半人工湖，原是一块沼泽地。公元1153年，金国定都燕京（后改称“中都”）后，金主在此修建金山行宫。后来，金章宗派人将西面玉泉山的水引到金山脚下，使它成为一处贮水池，称“金海”。元朝时，水利学家郭守敬主

are protected by pavilions built on top. Although weathered over hundreds of years, the writings are still legible, which describe the historical events of how the Ming Dynasty officials built ships to transport soldiers and supplies, the construction of the Dragon Temple and strikes of soldiers and migrant workers. The inscriptions played an important role in the study of the local history.

Kunming Lake

The Summer Palace in Beijing Haidian District is the largest and the best-

• 颐和园昆明湖
Kunming Lake in the Summer Palace

十七孔桥
Seventeen-arch Bridge

持将昌平的泉水和玉泉山的泉水注入湖中，改称“瓮山泊”。明代，湖中种植荷花，湖旁修建寺院、亭台，酷似江南风景。到了清代，乾隆帝将瓮山泊凿深并加以开拓，又根据汉武帝在长安都城凿昆明池操练水师的典故，将其命名为“昆明湖”，此名沿用至今。昆明湖背山面城，北宽南窄，形状犹如人的心脏。湖周长约15千米，面积约2平方千米。湖面波光粼粼，堤坝蜿蜒曲折，岛屿错落有致，各式建筑隐现其中，形成了以水为主体的颐和园美景。湖面上有一座长堤，名“西堤”，是仿杭州西湖的苏堤而建。西堤与另一小堤将湖面分

preserved existing imperial garden in China, mainly composed of Longevity Hill (*Wanshou Shan*) and Kunming Lake. Kunming Lake at the southern foot of Longevity Hill is a semi-natural and semi-artificial lake. Originally a marshland, Emperor Wanyan liang of the Jin Dynasty built a so-called Gold Mountain Palace on the hill in 1153 when he decided to establish his capital in Beijing. Later Emperor Zhang of the Jin Dynasty ordered to divert the water from Mount Yuquan (Jade Spring) near Beijing to the foot of the hills to create a pool named "Golden Sea" to store water. During the Yuan Dynasty, hydrologist Guo Shoujing supervised the project to divert spring water from Mount Yuquan and a nearby village into Golden Water River and he changed its name to Jug Mountain Lake. In the Ming Dynasty, lotuses were planted in the lake and temples and pavilions were built along the lakeside making the place almost like the landscape in the south of the Yangtze River. During the Qing Dynasty, Emperor Qianlong commissioned the work to dredge and expand Jug Mountain Lake and later named it Kunming Lake based on the story about Emperor Wu of the Han Dynasty training his imperial navy

为三部分，并各有一岛，分别为南湖岛、治镜阁岛和藻鉴堂岛。

其中南湖岛是昆明湖中最大的岛屿，岛上有涵虚堂和广润灵雨祠。涵虚堂是仿照湖北武汉的黄鹤楼建造而成的，慈禧太后曾在此检阅水师学堂的官兵演练。广润灵雨祠俗称“龙王庙”，与湖最南端的凤凰楼相对，寓意“龙凤呈祥”。

昆明湖边的清晏舫

昆明湖西岸边，有一只由汉白玉石制成的石舫，它本是乾隆时的旧物。慈禧重建颐和园时，在原船上加盖了两层西洋式楼阁，增设机轮，舱内墁花砖，镶嵌五色玻璃，陈设西洋桌椅，取名“清晏舫”。

Qingyan Fang beside Kunming Lake

On the west bank of Kunming Lake, there laid a boat made of white marble which was left from Emperor Qian Long's reign. When Cixi (Empress Dowager) rebuilt the Summer Palace, two storeys of western styles building and wheels were added to it. The floor inside the cabin is paved with tiles, and the walls are beset with stained glass. It is furnished with foreign style chairs and tables and given the name "*Qingyan Fang*".

on Kunming Lake in Chang'an (today's Xi'an). The name Kunming Lake has been used till the present day. The heart-shaped Kunming Lake is wider in the north and narrower in the south covering 2 square kilometers with a circumference of 15 kilometers. The scenic beauty of the Summer Palace with the water as the main theme is fully demonstrated by the landscape of a rippling lake, winding causeways, an interesting layout of the islands and a variety of building structures hidden in between. The West Causeway (*Xidi*) is modeled after the Su Causeway of the West Lake in Hangzhou. Together with another smaller causeway, the West Causeway separates the lake surface into three sections, each with an island. They are the South Lake Island(*Nanhu Dao*), the Mirror of Government Tower Island (*ZhiJingge Dao*) and the Hall of Recognition of Talent Island (*Zaojiantang Dao*).

The South Lake Island is the largest island on Kunming Lake. On the island are *Hanxu* Hall (Hall of Embracing the Universe) and *Guangrun Lingyu* Temple (Temple of Timely Rain and Moisture). The Hanxu Hall was modeled after the Yellow Crane Tower (*Huanghe Lou*) of Wuhan, Hubei Province. Empress

• 铜牛
Bronze Ox

仿北京卢沟桥而建的十七孔桥横跨在南湖岛和东堤之间，桥长150米，像一道长虹横跨在碧波之上。桥东湖岸上矗立的八角亭是中国古典园林中最大的一座观景亭，面积约300平方米，人们在此视野开阔，观景自如，所以得名“廓如亭”。亭附近蹲卧着一座如真牛大小的铜牛，此铜牛是镇水之物，用来防止水患。乾隆皇帝曾撰写《金牛铭》刻于金牛背上，现今仍可浏览观摩。昆明湖的西岸边，有一座白石舫，名清晏舫。舫体用巨大的白石雕造，上有两层舱楼，五色玻璃镶嵌其上，大方美观。

Dowager Cixi once reviewed the drills by the imperial naval academy in the hall. Commonly known as the Dragon King Temple, the Guangrun Lingyu Temple stands opposite the Phoenix Tower at the southern end of the lake, this layout implying good fortune from both the dragon and the phoenix. The 150-meter long Seventeen-Arch Bridge modeled after Beijing Lugou Bridge spans across the South Lake Island and the East Dyke. The octagonal-shaped Spacious Pavilion (*Kuoru Ting*) to the east of the bridge is the largest vista structure in ancient Chinese gardens with an area of 300 square meters. One can enjoy a panoramic view of Summer Palace from the pavilion. Crouching near the pavilion is a life-size bronze ox, which was believed to have the power to prevent flooding. Inscribed on the back of the ox is an ode entitled *Inscriptions on the Golden Ox* written by Emperor Qianlong. The inscriptions are still legible for viewing and studying. On the west bank of Kunming Lake stands the Clear and Peaceful Boat (*Qingyan Fang*) made of huge white rocks. The elegant-looking boat has two floors and colored glass mosaic on the windows.

西堤六桥

昆明湖西堤上建有六座石桥，它们造型优美，形态各异。这六座桥从北到南依次为界湖桥、豳风桥、玉带桥、镜桥、练桥和柳桥，合称“西堤六桥”。

Six Bridges on the West Causeway

The are six beautiful bridges of unique styles On the West Causeway of Kunming Lake. From north to south they are Lake-Dividing Bridge (*Jiehu Qiao*), Bridge of Pastoral Poems (*Binfeng Qiao*), Jade Belt Bridge (*Yudai Qiao*), Mirror Bridge (*Jing Qiao*), White Silk Bridge (*Lian Qiao*) and Willow Bridge (*Liu Qiao*).

- **界湖桥**

  界湖桥始建于乾隆年间，位于西堤的最北端，因其分界昆明湖内外湖与后溪河而得名。

  Lake-Dividing Bridge

  Originally built during Emperor Qianlong's reign, the bridge is located at the very northern end of the causeway and was named based on its location which divides the inner and outer Kunming Lake from the Houxi River.

- **柳桥**

  柳桥在西堤最南端，桥名取自诗句“柳桥晴有絮”。

  Willow Bridge

  The Willow Bridge at the very southern end of the West Causeway got its name from a poem describing willow catkins at the Willow Bridge on a nice day.

- **豳风桥**

初名桑苧桥，光绪帝时改为豳风桥。“豳风”取自中国第一部诗歌总集《诗经》十五国风之一的“豳风”，表明了古代帝王对农业的重视。

Bridge of Pastoral Poems

This bridge was originally named the Mulberry and Ramie Bridge. It was changed to Bridge of Pastoral Poems (*Binfeng Qiao*) during Emperor Guanxu's reign. The present name came from *The Book of Songs*, the first songbook in China. This demonstrates the great attention that ancient emperors paid to agriculture.

- **玉带桥**

玉带桥建造于乾隆年间，桥拱高而薄。桥身、桥栏皆用青白石和汉白玉石雕砌而成，弧形线条流畅，宛若玉带，故得此名。

Jade Belt Bridge

Built during Emperor Qianlong's reign, this high-arched narrow bridge was named Jade Belt Bridge because its body and railings are made of gray white and white marbles, and the chape of the bridge resembles a jade belt.

镜桥

镜桥始建于乾隆年间，光绪时重建。桥名出自唐代诗人李白“两水夹明镜，双桥落彩虹”的诗句。

Mirror Bridge

Originally built during Emperor Qianlong's reign and rebuilt during Emperor Guangxu's reign, this bridge got its name from a verse by Li Bai, a great poet of the Tang Dynasty, who wrote: "A bright mirror between two pieces of water, a rainbow falls over the two bridges."

练桥

桥名出自诗句“余霞散成绮，澄江静如练”。桥上建有四角重檐桥亭，此处视野开阔，南湖岛、十七孔桥、佛香阁建筑群尽收眼底。此桥主要供游人观景和憩息。

White Silk Bridge

The name of the bridge came from a poet that compares both the sunset set glow and the tranquility of the water to silk. A pavilion built with double eaves on four roof corners provides a resting place for visitors and a panoramic view of South Lake Island, Seventeen-Arch Bridge and Buddha Fragrance Tower building structures.

什刹海

什刹海位于北京西北隅、北海公园北门附近，是一处人工湖泊。湖面积34万平方米，元代称海子。元朝建筑师曾依托这一水域在湖东岸确定了都城建设的中轴线，当时它还是南北大运河的终点码头，船运业极为繁盛。明清时期，湖面缩小，形成西海、后海、前海三个相连的湖泊，湖边盖起了许多亭园小楼。什刹海又称十刹海，因周围有

Shichahai

Shichahai (Shicha Lake) is an artificial lake of 340,000 square meters near the north gate of Beihai Park, northwest of Beijing. It was called *Haizi* in the Yuan Dynasty. The Yuan engineers examined the location of the lake and determined that the central axis for the city was at the east shore of the lake. It was once the Grand Canal's terminal with a very prosperous shipping industry. During the Ming and Qing dynasties, as the

• 什刹海
Shichahai

什刹海夜色
Night at *Shichahai*

十座古寺而得名，后逐渐成为人们的游乐消夏之地。

什刹海周围树木葱茏，湖面平静，风光秀丽。银锭桥位于后海与前海之间的水道上，因形状似银锭而得名。银锭桥以西，垂柳摇曳多姿，站在桥上既可北望后海，又可遥望西山美景，故有“银锭观山”的说法。

什刹海不仅自然景观优美，而且与人文胜地交相辉映。恭王府位于什刹海西北角，建于18世纪末，

lake surface area became smaller, there appeared three connected lakes of West Lake (*Xihai*), Back Lake (*Houhai*) and Front Lake (*Qianhai*). Pavilions and small buildings were built along the lakeside gradually making this area a place of leisure especially in the summer. *Shichahai* is also known as the Lake of Ten Temples because of the nearby ten ancient temples.

Shichahai is well-known for its scenic beauty of surrounding lush trees and tranquility of the lake. Between the Back Lake and the Front Lake stands Yinding Bridge (Silver Ingot Bridge) named after its silver ingot shape. Standing on the bridge one can enjoy a view of willow trees and distant mountains to the west and scenery of the Back Lake to the north, hence the saying "view mountains from Yinding".

Not only famous for its beautiful natural scenery, *Shichahai* also has many historical and cultural attractions. Prince Gong's Mansion located at the northwest corner was built at the end of the 18th century and is considered the best-preserved royal mansions of the Qing Dynasty in Beijing. It was originally the residence of He Shen, the grand councilor for Emperor Qianlong of the Qing Dynasty and later bestowed to Prince Gong. The

恭王府花园诗画舫

诗画舫位于方塘东岸，廊两侧为宽阔的水面，是一条长长的游廊，主要作赏荷垂钓、吟诗作画之用。

Corridor of Poems and Paintings in Prince Gong's Mansion

The long corridor is located to the east of the square pond with water on both sides. It was used mainly for viewing lotus flowers, fishing, painting and reading poems.

是北京保存最完整的清代王府。这里原是清朝乾隆时期大学士和珅的府邸，后被赐予恭亲王奕䜣。恭王府分为宅邸和花园两部分。宅邸由多个四合院构成，分东、中、西三路。东路的乐道堂是当年恭亲王奕䜣的起居之处；中路的殿堂顶部全部覆有绿色琉璃瓦，威严气派；西路院落小巧精致，内部雕饰精美绝伦。花园又名萃锦园，也分中、

entire compound is divided into the living quarter and the garden. The living quarter is composed of multiple courtyards in the east, center and west of the compound. Prince Gong lived in "*Ledao Tang*" (Hall of Enjoying Sage Teachings) in an east-side courtyard. The center of the compound consists of majestic halls with green glazed tile roofs. The west-side courtyards are smaller and delicate with elegant decorations. The garden

东、西三路，东路以建筑为主，大戏台坐落在此；中路是花园建筑主体，入口处有西洋风格的汉白玉石拱门；西路以山水为主，大方池位于中心位置，池中有一个方形小岛，岛上有观鱼台。

东平湖

东平湖位于山东省西部东平县境内，东连大汶河，西依京杭大运河，南临曲阜，北通黄河。宋金时这里称梁山泊，元明时称鞍山湖，

Cuijin Yuan is also divided into central, east and west sections. The east side is mainly occupied by buildings including the Grand Opera House. A western-style white marble arch gate stands at the entrance of the main garden section in the center. The landscape in the west side includes a big square pond with a small island in the center and a pavilion named *Guanyu Tai* on the island.

Dongping Lake

Dongping Lake is situated in Dongping County, west of Shandong Province

东平湖（图片提供：全景正片）
Dongping Lake

从腊山山顶俯瞰东平湖（图片提供：FOTOE）
Overlooked from the Top of Mount Lashan to Dongping Lake

清咸丰年间命名为东平湖。原来的东平湖是一个常年蓄水的浅水湖，湖面面积只有153平方千米。后来东平湖水库修建成功，使湖面面积扩展到627平方千米，蓄水量达40亿立方米，东平湖一跃成为山东省第二大淡水湖泊。

腊山位于东平湖西畔，与东平湖山水相依，其主峰海拔为258.4米，素有“山奇雄，峰奇秀，岩奇险，石奇美”之称，自古被誉为“小泰山”。周围72座山峰各有特色，其中小岱峰以其悬崖陡峭、奇

connecting to Dawen River to the east, the Beijing-Hangzhou Grand Canal to the west, Yellow River to the north and Qufu to the south. It was called Liangshan Lake during the Song and Jin dynasties, and Anshan Lake during the Yuan and Ming dynasties. It was officially named Dongping Lake in Emperor Xianfeng's reign. Originally a shallow lake of 153 square kilometers for annual water impoundment, Dongping Lake was expanded to 627 square kilometers with a water storage capacity of 4 billion cubic meters and became the second largest freshwater lake in Shandong Province when Dongping reservoir was completed.

Located to the west of the neighboring Dongping Lake, Mount Lashan is well known for its unique beauty of cliffs, rocks and trees. That is how Mount Lashan got the name of "little Mount Taishan". Its main peak has an elevation of 258.4 meters. Of the surrounding 72 mountain peaks, Xiaodai Peak is famous for its precipices and many strange-looking pine trees.

Dongping Lake is the only lake

《水浒传》

《水浒传》又名《忠义水浒传》，一般简称《水浒》，是中国古代四大名著之一。作者施耐庵，元末明初的文学家。全书描写了北宋末年以宋江为首的一百零八位好汉聚义梁山，凭借水泊地势天险，替天行道，除暴安良，以及接受招安、四处征战的故事。

Outlaws of the Marsh

Outlaws of the Marsh, also known as *Water Margin* is one of the four great classics of Chinese ancient literature written by Shi Nai'an between the end of the Yuan Dynasty and the beginning of the Ming Dynasty. The novel tells the story of how 108 outlaws headed by Song Jiang met in Mount Liangshan and used the lake's terrain as barriers to kill the corrupted government officials for the poor. They were eventually granted amnesty and sent on to fight battles for the government.

松、怪柏众多而一枝独秀。

东平湖是《水浒传》中八百里水泊唯一遗存的水域。宋朝时期，梁山好汉们以水泊为屏障，杀富济贫，除暴安良，替天行道，演绎了一场轰轰烈烈的农民起义壮举。东平湖中有一座小岛，呈椭圆形，是《水浒传》中水浒英雄们的栖身之地，所以也称“聚义岛”。

existing today in "the eight hundreds *Li* of lakes" described in the famous Chinese literature classic *Outlaws of the Marsh*. During a peasant uprising in the Song Dynasty, a group of outlaws got together and took advantage of the lake's terrain to fight against the corrupted government for the poor and the weak. A small oval-shaped island in Dongping Lake was the place where these outlaws were often seen, hence the name Juyi Island (island of meeting for justice).

玄武湖

玄武湖位于江苏省南京市东北城墙外，西临明朝定都时修建的城

Xuanwu Lake

Xuanwu Lake is located outside of

• **玄武湖**

“玄武”是中国神话故事中的四象之一，是龟与蛇的复合体，青龙、白虎、朱雀、玄武分别代表着东、西、南、北四个方位的神。“玄武”意为“北方之神”， 其实玄武湖实际上就是“北湖”的意思。

Xuanwu Lake

Xuanwu is one of the Four Symbols in the Chinese mythology, each of which represents a direction, Black Dragon of the east, White Tiger of the west, Red Sparrow of the south and Xuanwu of the north. Xuanwu, the God of North, has a body of both a snake and a turtle. Xuanwu Lake actually means the Lake of North.

门玄武门，东邻紫金山，三面环山，一面紧靠古老的南京城垣。它古称“桑泊”，是一块因断层作用而形成的沼泽湿地，相传三国时期吴王孙权引水成湖，在这里训练水师，取名“练湖”。南朝宋时，湖上开始修建林苑亭阁，并改名为“玄武湖”。玄武湖是中国古

northeast city walls of Nanjing, Jiangsu Province bordering Xuanwu Gate built in the Ming Dynasty capital to the west and Zijin Mountain to the east. Surrounded by mountains in three sides and next to the landmark of ancient Nanjing, it was once a wetland formed in the fault movement. During the Three Kingdoms Period, Sun Quan, the King of State Wu, decided to

代最大的皇家湖泊园林，也是当代仅存的江南皇家园林。

玄武湖湖区广阔，湖岸呈菱形，湖周长有10千米，水面约3.95平方千米。玄武湖形似火腿，湖泊分为北湖(东北湖、西北湖)、东南湖及西南湖，西南湖水最深，东南湖次之，北湖水较浅。湖上有五个小岛，即环洲、樱洲、菱洲、梁洲和翠洲，五岛之间以堤桥相连。环洲像两只巨大的手臂从南北两边伸向湖中，素有“环洲烟柳”之称。

divert water into the wetland to train his navy, hence the name *Lian Hu* (Practice Lake for Training). Starting from the Song of the Southern dynasties, gardens and pavilions were built and the name was changed to Xuanwu Lake. It is the largest imperial water garden of ancient China and the only imperial garden existing today south of the Yangtze River.

Xuanwu Lake with a vast area, has a rhombus-shaped lakeside covering an area of 3.95 square kilometers

• 古阅武台（图片提供：FOTOE）
Ancient Pavilion of Martial Arts

环洲正对玄武门的拐角处有一座假山，假山旁有两块形状奇特的太湖石，一块形似观音，一块形似童子，故名“童子拜观音”。

梁洲是五座小岛中开辟最早、风景最佳的地方，又名“美洲”，原为梁代昭明太子（501—531）读书处，因传说梁昭明太子萧统曾在此建有“梁园”，同文人学士一起赋诗唱和，故称“梁洲”，有“梁洲秋菊”的美誉。翠洲环境清

梁园（图片提供：全景正片）
Liangyuan Garden

with a circumference of 10 kilometers. The surface area is shaped like a pig's hind leg and divided into the northeast lake, northwest lake, southeast lake and southwest lake. The southwest lake has the deepest water and southeast lake is the second deepest lake. The lakes in the north have relatively shallower water. There are five small islets (*Huan Zhou, Ying Zhou, Ling Zhou, Liang Zhou and Cui Zhou*) connected by bridges and dykes. *Huan Zhou* resembles two huge arms extending to the center of the lake from the north and the south. It is known for its scenery of "Willows in Fog Island". Around the corner facing Xuanwu Gate stands a manmade hill with two grotesque Taihu Lake stones, one like *Guanyin* (Avalokitesvara) and one like a child, hence the name "Child Paying Respect to *Guanyin*" for the rocks.

Among the five islets, *Liang Zhou* was built first and has the best scenery, which makes it known as "the Islet of Beauty". Originally a place where Prince Zhaoming of Liang Dynasty (501-531) studied, it is said that he built the Liangyuan Garden here to write and chant poems with his fellow scholars, hence the name "*Liang Zhou*" (Liang Islet). Chrysanthemum in autumn is a major attraction of Liang Islet. *Cui Zhou*(Green Islet) has a secluded

幽，树木葱茏，有“翠洲云树”之称。樱洲位于环洲怀抱之中，昔日樱桃遍布洲上，故而得名，有“樱洲花海”之誉。菱洲处于玄武湖中心位置，与翠洲南北遥遥相对，因这里过去多产菱角，故名“菱洲”。在菱洲上可观赏钟山山顶上千变万化的云霞，故称“菱洲山岚”。

瘦西湖

瘦西湖位于江苏省扬州市西北

tranquil environment full of lushly green trees known as "Cui Zhou Towering Trees". Embraced by *Huan Zhou* (Loop Islet), *Ying Zhou* (Cherry Islet) was once covered with cherry trees known as "Sea of Flowers of Cherry Islet". *Ling Zhou* (Water Chestnut Islet), located in the center of Xuanwu Lake and facing the distant Cui Zhou, was named after water chestnuts produced here in the past. Ling Zhou also provides the best view of ever-changing mysterious fog and clouds during sunrise and sunset on top of Zhongshan Mountain in the distance,

• 瘦西湖
Slender West Lake

• 虹桥
Rainbow Bridge

部，清瘦狭长，窈窕曲折，呈“L”形，水面长约5000米，宽不及100米，故称“瘦西湖”。瘦西湖原是扬州城外一条保障河，明清时期，当地豪绅争相在此整修水面，疏浚河道，修筑水上园林，使其成为达官贵人挥金如土、纸醉金迷的乐园。

瘦西湖的美主要在于蜿蜒曲折，古朴多姿。它窈窕清瘦，串以虹桥、五亭桥、小金山、白塔、二十四桥等风景、建筑，俨然一幅天然秀美的国画长卷，自古以来使是游览胜地。小金山位于湖区西北隅，是瘦西湖最大的岛屿，由历代

hence the name "*Ling Zhou* Misty Mountain".

Slender West Lake

Slender West Lake (*Shou Xi Hu*) is located to the northwest of Yangzhou City, Jiangsu Province, named after its long and slender "L" shape and its resemblance to the West Lake in Hangzhou. It is 5,000 meters long and less than 100 meters wide. Originally a crisscrossed river outside of Yangzhou, it was dredged and expanded during the Ming and Qing dynasties by local gentry, who built gardens and pavilions around the lake making it a retreat for dignitaries and the rich of lavish lifestyle.

The beauty of Slender West Lake lies in its winding watercourse meandered through the scenic landscape of Rainbow Bridge, Five Pavilion Bridge, Small Golden Hill, White Pagoda and Twenty-four Bridge. Resembling a natural and elegant long Chinese scroll painting, it has always been a tourist attraction since ancient times. The Small Golden Hill to the north of the lake is the largest island on the lake built on sediments as a result of several generations of dredge work. It has many cultural relics and historical

挖湖后的淤泥堆积而成。小金山上文物古迹众多。山顶建有风亭，是眺景最佳处。

“扬州好，第一是虹桥”。虹桥横跨于瘦西湖上，始建于明代崇祯年间，原为木桥，因两侧围以红色扶栏，当时名为“红桥”。后改建为三孔石桥，如同横卧于湖面上的彩虹，故改称“虹桥”。虹桥西边有一座修筑于隋代的柳堤，每至春季，堤上杨柳依依，景色优美，清代无数文人雅士来此赏景游玩，并写下许多名文诗作。

五亭桥又名“莲花桥”，位于瘦西湖莲性寺的莲花堤上。因桥上

• 五亭桥
Five Pavilion Bridge

sites. The best vista point is the pavilion built on top of the hill.

The Rainbow Bridge (*Hong Qiao*) stands across the southern mouth of the lake known as the best scenic spot in Yangzhou. Originally built during Emperor Chongzhen of the Ming Dynasty, it was a wooden bridge named "Red Bridge" after its red railings on both sides. During the Emperor Qianlong's reign of the Qing Dynasty, the bridge was rebuilt into a three-arch stone bridge resembling a rainbow over the lake. So the character "red" changed to the character for rainbow with the same pronunciation. To the west of the bridge is a causeway built in the Sui Dynasty and planted with many willow trees. Every spring when the scenery was at its best, numerous literary figures of the Qing Dynasty visited here leaving behind many noted poems and literary works.

Five Pavilion Bridge (*Wuting Qiao*), also known as Lotus Bridge, spans the Lotus Causeway near the Lotus Temple. The bridge got its name from the five pavilions built on the top of the bridge deck with the largest pavilion in the center and two smaller ones on each side. Supported by red pillars, the five pavilions are connected to each other

建有五座亭子，故名“五亭桥”。居中为一座大亭，四翼各有一座小亭，五亭均有红色的柱子支撑，亭与亭之间有游廊相连，并设有坐凳栏杆。亭顶覆有黄色琉璃瓦，亭角飞翘，亭内有彩绘藻井，显得富丽堂皇。桥墩由12块大青石砌成，形成厚重有力的“工”字形桥基，有15个大小不一、形状不同的桥洞。中国著名桥梁专家茅以升曾评价：中国最具艺术美的桥就是扬州的五亭桥。

through corridors with seating along the railings. The yellow glazed-tile roofs with the upturned corners and painted ceilings give the five pavilions a splendid look. Each bridge pier is made of 12 large pieces of bluestones. The strong and heavy I-shaped bridge foundation supports 15 arches of different sizes and shapes. The famous Chinese bridge expert Mao Yisheng once commended that Five Pavilion Bridge embodies the most artistic beauty among all bridges in China.

千岛湖

千岛湖实际上就是新安江水库，位于浙江省杭州西郊的淳安县境内。1960年，新安江水库建成，水域面积达580平方千米，连绵的崇山峻岭淹入湖中成为大小岛屿，常见岛屿有398个，低水位时岛屿逾千，故名“千岛湖”。它是世界上岛屿最多的湖。

千岛湖呈树枝型分布，群岛分布有疏有密。在岛屿群集处，众岛似连非连，湖面被分隔得宽窄不同，犹如迷宫一般；岛屿稀疏处，湖面开阔浩渺，一碧万顷。湖中的小

Thousand Island Lake

Thousand Island Lake (*Qiandao Hu*) is in fact the Xin'an River Reservoir located in Chun'an County west of Hangzhou, Zhejiang Province. The reservoir was completed in 1960 covering an area of 580 square kilometers. Hills upon hills were submerged under the water, so there are 398 islands are commonly seen and over 1,000 islands can be seen at low water level. It is the lake that has the largest number of islands in the world, hence the name "Thousand Island Lake".

The islands are distributed like branches on a tree, densely in some locations and sparsely in others. In areas

岛会随着湖水的涨落时大时小，时有时无。千岛湖湖水清碧如玉，不经任何处理即可达到饮用水标准。

千岛湖南岸最主要的景色是石林，景区内奇石遍布，石峰、石笋、石柱，栩栩如生，犹如进入仙境一般。如玳瑁岭的狮子林，数十只大小不同的狮子，坐、卧、跑、跳，形态各异，令人叫绝。

where islands are concentrated, the lake surface is divided into small pieces as if they were puzzles. But in areas where islands spread out thinly, the lake seems open and vast. Small islands in the lake become smaller or bigger, visible or hidden with the rise and fall of the lake tides. The water in the lake is so clear that it meets drinking water standard without any treatment.

• **千岛湖**（图片提供：全景正片）
Thousand Island Lake

• 海瑞
Hai Rui

龙山位于千岛湖的中心，面积0.45平方千米，因形似苍龙而得名。龙山上有海瑞祠，祠为重檐歇山式结构，威武庄严。海瑞（1514—1587）是明朝著名的清官，为政清廉，洁身自爱，为人正直刚毅，忠心耿耿，深得民众爱戴。海瑞的全身塑像立于正堂，祠内有海瑞遗迹陈列室，回廊中有“去思碑”和纪念海瑞的诗碑。蜜山岛位于湖区东南方向，面积0.36平方千米，山巅西侧有蜜山泉，水质甘洌，四季不竭。

The key attraction on the southern lakeside is the giant forest of limestone rocks. This area is full of stone peaks, stone columns and stalagmites. The stone forest in Mount Turtle (*Daimao Ling*) has rocks shaped in lifelike lions of different sizes in different postures of sitting, lying, running and jumping. This amazing world of stone forests makes the visitors feel that they entered a fairyland.

Mount Dragon (*Long Shan*) in the center of the lake covers 0.45 square kilometers and is named after its dragon shape. The solemn Hai Rui Memorial Hall of double eaves is located on this mountain. Hai Rui was an official in the Ming Dynasty famous for his honesty, integrity, fairness and uncompromising adherence to upright morality. He was well-liked by common people. The memorial has a full-length statue of Hai Rui in the main hall, an exhibition room and some steles of poems and inscriptions in memory of him. Mishan Island is located southeast of the lake covering an area of in the 0.36 square kilometers. On the west side of the mountain is a spring of sweet and clear water running all year around.

星湖

星湖位于广东省肇庆市市区北部，湖、岩交错，点缀如星，故名“星湖”。星湖原为天然沼泽区，湖底有涌泉，后经治理、开辟、改

Star Lake

Star Lake (*Xing Hu*) is situated in north Zhaoqing, Guangdong Province dotted with many crags. The interlaced crags in the lake resemble stars in the sky, hence the name Star Lake. It was originally

星湖（图片提供：全景正片）
Star Lake

造，成为风景秀丽的浩瀚平湖。湖堤总长20多千米，湖面约6平方千米，整个湖面被蜿蜒交错的湖堤划分为6部分，各湖之间有堤桥相连。山崖、湖堤间还建有40多座亭台楼阁。

湖滨有7座石灰岩山，排列如北斗七星，故称“七星岩”。它们大多是天然洞穴，毫无人工斧凿的痕迹。天柱岩为最高峰，海拔114米。

a natural marshland with spring water underneath and became a scenic lake after many constructions and water treatments. The lake covers 6 square kilometers with over 20-kilometer long crisscrossed embankment dividing the lake surface area into six connected sections. There are more than 40 pavilions and terraces built between the crags on the embankment.

Seven limestone crags on the lakeside stand in the natural formation of "the Big Dipper" layout and thus are named "Seven Star Crags". They are mainly natural caves without any traces of human chisels. The Heavenly Pillar Crag (*Tianzhu Yan*) is the highest with an elevation of 114 meters. The Rock Chamber Crag has the most cultural relics with the crag top named "Song Tai" (chanting platform) where the god hosted a banquet for deities and immortals according to legends. Below the crag is a huge cave with a 2-meter high

• 七星岩摩崖石刻（图片提供：FOTOE）
Cliff Inscriptions of Seven Star Crags

石室岩为名胜古迹集中之处，岩顶名“嵩台”，相传是天帝宴请百神之所。岩下有一特大石室洞，洞口高2米，洞内高达30多米，石乳、石柱、石幔遍布其中，摩崖石刻共有270多处。如石室洞口石壁上的唐代李邕写的《端州石室记》，具体而形象地描述了他进入石室洞之后的神奇感受。石室洞南口左侧有一座宫殿式建筑，始建于明代，名“水月宫”，宫内原有许多造型优美的仙女像，只可惜已经被毁。水月宫旁湖面上有一组水亭，中间为一座八角重檐亭，它的四面各有一座四角单檐亭，呈放射式排列状，合称“五龙亭”。

这里还保留着大量隋唐、明清时期的古村落。如位于星湖西北方向的杨池古村，村内古屋为硬山顶或悬山顶建筑，清一色的砖木结构，墙壁上有精美的壁画、灰塑和木雕。村落巷道如梳齿般纵向排列，祠堂、书院、花厅、磨坊，甚至钱庄、银库等中国古代城镇特有的景观星罗棋布。

entrance and a over 30-meter high ceiling inside full of stalactites of various shapes. There are over 270 cliff inscriptions such as the amazing impressions of the cave written by Li Yong of the Tang Dynasty at the cave's entrance. At the southern exit of the cave stands a palace-style structure originally built in the Ming Dynasty called "Palace of Clear Moon", which used to contain statues of beautiful fairies, but was destroyed unfortunately. On the lake next to the palace is a series of water pavilions with a double-eave, octagonal pavilion in the middle extended on each of the four sides by a single-eave, quadrangular pavilion. This group of pavilions is called "Five Dragon Pavilions".

A large number of ancient villages from the Sui, Tang, Ming and Qing dynasties are well-preserved around the lake such as Yangchi Village to the northwest of Star Lake. The houses in the village are all made of bricks and timber with overhanging roofs, exquisite murals, lime sculptures and wood carvings. The streets in the village are neatly laid out in a vertical direction. The village has all the characteristics of a Chinese ancient town including an ancestral hall, a school, a mill and even a bank and a treasury.